Perfectly Brilliant

KNITS

MELISSA MATTHAY
AND SHERYL THIES

Martingale®
& COMPANY

Perfectly Brilliant Knits
© 2005 by Melissa Matthay and Sheryl Thies

Martingale®
& COMPANY

Martingale & Company
20205 144th Avenue NE
Woodinville, WA 98072-8478 USA
www.martingale-pub.com

CREDITS

President: Nancy J. Martin
CEO: Daniel J. Martin
VP and General Manager: Tom Wierzbicki
Publisher: Jane Hamada
Editorial Director: Mary V. Green
Managing Editor: Tina Cook
Technical Editor: Ursula Reikes
Copy Editor: Liz McGehee
Design Director: Stan Green
Illustrator: Robin Strobel
Cover and Text Designer: Shelly Garrison
Photographer: Brent Kane
Photo Stylists: Shelly Garrison and Robin Strobel

Printed in China
10 09 08 07 06 05   8 7 6 5 4 3 2 1

Library of Congress Cataloging-in-Publication Data

Matthay, Melissa.
    Perfectly brilliant knits / Melissa Matthay
        and Sheryl Thies. p. cm.
    ISBN 1-56477-594-1
    1. Knitting—Patterns. 2. Sweaters. I. Thies,
Sheryl. II. Title.
    TT825.M32 2005
    746.43'20432—dc22
                                    2005003482

MISSION STATEMENT
Dedicated to providing quality products and
service to inspire creativity.

DEDICATION

For Aaron and Dylan; Amos and Ursula.
Remember, it takes courage to share your dreams with others.

Melissa with her sons, Aaron and Dylan, at the Knitting Tree.

Contents

Introduction

Welcome to *Perfectly Brilliant Knits*, and congratulations on your interest in taking your knitting to the next level. If you like creating and wearing striking knit garments, you will enjoy this book.

For over 25 years, Melissa has been turning the latest yarns into contemporary and brilliantly knit clothing. She finds inspiration by working with customers at the Knitting Tree as well as by making return trips to New York City, where she owned a yarn shop for 20 years.

Melissa is known for her contemporary designs that can be completed in a practical amount of time. Her unique designs, surprising yarn combinations, and uncomplicated, easy-to-understand directions inspire and delight knitters. Wearing the garment in the same season it is started *is* possible, thanks to a reasonable stitch gauge of three or four stitches per inch.

Each project in this book includes an original design with a defining feature, trim, or pattern stitch that turns a basic sweater into brilliant attire. The Melissa's Points signal a bit of Melissa's humor and dramatic flair. Valuable information is provided in each Skill Builder to help you perfect your knitting technique.

Cross the bridge from basic and move up to brilliance. Turn your dreams into reality and enjoy the compliments you'll receive on your *Perfectly Brilliant Knits*.

Unraveling Some Mysteries

At the core of knitting are some basic techniques: casting on, knitting, purling, and binding off. Combining these basic techniques with the appropriate tools and materials might seem a little overwhelming. Unravel some of the mystery. Understand how yarn and needles impact gauge, realize the importance of gauge, and create a garment that fits. Expand your understanding, unleash your creative spirit, and create *Perfectly Brilliant Knits*.

SELECTING YARN

Ideally, once you've decided on a project, the specified yarn is available. In reality, this may not be the case. The yarn may not be available for many reasons. You may prefer a color that is not available; there may not be enough yarn in stock, or it is not stocked at all. You may prefer a different fiber due to climate, or the yarn may be discontinued. Each season, manufacturers produce many new yarns and discontinue other yarns.

Whatever your reason, substituting one yarn for another can easily be done, provided you make an informed decision. The critical factor is gauge; the gauge stated in the pattern must be achieved for the garment to fit. The yarn label will recommend a gauge and needle size for the yarn, but doing a swatch is still necessary (see "Making a Gauge Swatch" on page 8).

The Craft Yarn Council of America has developed standards to make substituting easier. Yarn weight is indicated by a yarn-skein symbol with a number between 1 and 6, with 1 being the finest and 6 being the thickest. This standardization is being implemented over time and should become a familiar icon in the future.

Combining yarns is an easy way to bulk up thinner yarns to achieve a specific gauge. The following chart will provide a guide for combining yarns to achieve a bulkier yarn. This is only a guide; do a swatch to be sure of your gauge.

GUIDE FOR COMBINING YARNS	
Yarn Combinations	Approximate New Gauge
Two DK-weight yarns	14 sts per 4"
One DK yarn and one worsted yarn	12 sts per 4"
Two worsted yarns	11 sts per 4"

YARN-WEIGHT SYMBOLS						
Yarn-Weight Symbol & Category Name	1 SUPER FINE	2 FINE	3 LIGHT	4 MEDIUM	5 BULKY	6 SUPER BULKY
Types of Yarns in Category	Sock, Fingering, Baby	Sport, Baby	DK, Light Worsted	Worsted, Afghan, Aran	Chunky, Craft, Rug	Bulky, Roving
Knit Gauge Ranges in Stockinette Stitch to 4"	27 to 32 sts	23 to 26 sts	21 to 24 sts	16 to 20 sts	12 to 15 sts	6 to 11 sts
Recommended Needle in U.S. Size Range	1 to 3	3 to 5	5 to 7	7 to 9	9 to 11	11 and larger

Working two yarns together will give the look of a totally new yarn and is one way to create a custom look. For a "rag" or flecked appearance, combine two flat, solid-colored yarns. Combining a flat and a nubby or slubbed yarn will give a new texture. Combining two textured yarns will give a new depth. Try mixing colors that at first glance don't go together; you may be pleasantly surprised. Go ahead and experiment; just do a gauge swatch.

When substituting one yarn for another, check the yardage; all balls and skeins are not created equal. Determine the total length of yarn required by multiplying the number of balls required by the yards per ball. Divide this number (total yardage required) by the yards per ball of the new yarn (listed on the label) to determine the number of balls of new yarn. Round up to the next whole number. For metric measurements, see "Yarn Conversion" on page 111.

Purchase enough yarn to complete the project. Check to be sure the dye lot is the same. The subtle differences may not seem noticeable while the yarn is in a ball but may become blatant once the garment is knit.

SELECTING NEEDLES

There are a variety of needles made from many different materials: bamboo, plastic, metal, ebony, and other hardwoods. Personal preference should rule. Some knitters prefer the click of metal needles; some prefer the slide of ebony. Basically, there are two types of needles: straight and circular. Straight needles are used for working back and forth across rows. Circular needles can be used to work around and around, creating a tube, as for a neckline. They can also be used the same as straight needles to work back and forth across rows; the connecting cable can be an advantage when working with a large number of stitches. The pattern will state when a circular needle is required.

When selecting needles, it is essential that you use the size that will give you the required gauge. The material from which the needle is made or the type, straight or circular, is a matter of personal choice. You may already have your favorites. Use what you are most comfortable with, provided the gauge is correct.

The pattern will call for a specific needle size and the yarn label will give a needle size. Consider this a starting point. The size of the stitch is determined in part by the diameter of the needle. Matching the needle size with the yarn and your unique knitting tension achieves the gauge. Going up or down one or two needle sizes is not uncommon.

MAKING A GAUGE SWATCH

The most critical factor to achieving the correct fit is gauge. Gauge simply means the number of stitches per inch. All patterns are based on a specific number of stitches per inch. If your knitting does not equal the specified number of stitches per inch, the garment will not fit. The size of the needle, the thickness of the yarn, and the knitter all influence gauge.

The size of the needle you actually use really doesn't matter. What matters is that you use a size that allows you to obtain the correct gauge. You may have to make several swatches with different-size needles to achieve the gauge stated in the pattern.

Make a swatch using the yarn for the project. If the garment has a pattern stitch, the swatch should have enough stitches to work across the pattern. If your garment is done in stockinette stitch, cast on about 4" worth of stitches. The gauge noted in the pattern and on the yarn label will indicate how many stitches that would be. Cast on and work in pattern for about 4".

Measure across the width of the swatch. Divide the number of stitches on the needle by the inches to determine the number of stitches per inch. If the number of stitches per inch is a larger number than you want, try a larger needle size and make a new swatch. If the number of stitches per inch is less than you want, go down a needle size. Continue to make swatches using different-size needles until you have the correct gauge.

Once you have achieved the correct stitch gauge, measure the number of rows per inch. Since the patterns in this collection are written with length given in inches instead of rows, the row gauge is less important than the stitch gauge. If you achieve stitch gauge without achieving row gauge, go with the needles that give the correct stitch gauge.

DETERMINING YOUR SIZE

Using a flexible tape measure, measure across the largest part of your bust and hips. Measure the desired length of the garment by holding a tape measure at the shoulder and determining where you would like the garment to end. Measure the width of the upper arm and wrist. Hold the tape measure at the top of the shoulder to determine the length of the sleeve.

Don't automatically rely on the terms Small, Medium, or Large. Instead, look at the finished bust measurements and the pattern-diagram measurements. The finished bust measurement represents the finished size of the completed garment. Compare these measurements to your body measurements, adding several inches for ease. Several inches of ease are required for a comfortable fit.

The number of additional inches is a matter of personal choice. A tight- to close-fitting garment may have 1" to 3" of ease. A more classic fit may have 4" to 6" of ease. And an oversized garment may have 6" to 10" or more of ease. Measuring a favorite sweater and comparing to your body measurements will give you an idea of the amount of ease you prefer. Select the garment size that gives enough ease for a comfortable fit.

BODY MEASUREMENTS
Bust
Hips
Desired length of garment
Circumference of wrist
Circumference of upper arm
Desired length of sleeve

ADJUSTING LENGTHS

Body length can easily be adjusted but must be done before reaching the armhole shaping. To shorten, just eliminate the desired number of inches on the front and back pieces. Subtract the same number of inches from the entire length of the piece. Lengthening the piece is the same process; make the adjustment before the armhole shaping. The length of the armhole will not be affected but the overall length will be.

Adjustments to sleeve length need to be made before the sleeve cap. An easy way of determining when to start the sleeve cap is to hold the knit sleeve to your arm. Once the sleeve is long enough to reach the top of your bra at the underarm, begin the cap shaping.

Color-Block Shell

*Look and feel great in this shell with cool,
water-colored blocks outlined in black.*

Skill Level: Easy ◖■□▷

Sizes: Extra Small (Small, Medium, Large, Extra Large)
Finished Bust: 37½ (39½, 41½, 43, 45)"

Skill Builder

Changing colors: To prevent holes, always pick up the new-color yarn
from beneath the dropped yarn and keep the color just worked to the left.

Melissa's Point

I got inspired when I received a purse as a gift and had to make a
matching top. Now if only I could find shoes to match.

COLOR-BLOCK SHELL

MATERIALS

A 1 skein of Victoria from S. Charles (60% cotton, 40% viscose; 50 g; 70 yds), color 12 🔳

B 2 (2, 2, 3, 3) skeins of Elena from Filatura di Crosa (100% Egyptian cotton; 50 g; 99 yds), color 3 🔳

C 2 (2, 2, 3, 3) skeins of Elena from Filatura di Crosa, color 5

D 2 (2, 2, 3, 3) skeins of Victoria from S. Charles, color 27

E 2 (2, 2, 3, 3) skeins of Victoria from S. Charles, color 32

Size 9 needles or size required to obtain gauge

Size 7 circular needles (24")

Size H crochet hook

GAUGE

17 sts and 21 rows = 4" in St st on larger needles

BACK

- With smaller needles and A, CO 80 (84, 88, 92, 96) sts and knit 1 row (WS row).

- Change to larger needles and B, beg St st: K40 (42, 44, 46, 48), drop B but do not cut yarn. Add C, K40 (42, 44, 46, 48). Work in St st and established colors until piece measures 10 (11, 12, 13, 13)", ending with purl row.

- Change to A and knit 1 row. Change to D, cont in St st: Work 40 (42, 44, 46, 48) sts, drop D but do not cut yarn. Add E and work 40 (42, 44, 46, 48) sts. Cont in St st and established color until piece measures 11 (12, 13, 14, 14)", ending with WS row.

- **Shape armholes:** BO 5 (5, 6, 6, 7) sts at beg of next 2 rows, dec 1 st at each edge EOR 6 (7, 8, 10, 10) times—58 (60, 60, 60, 62) sts. Cont in patt until piece measures 15½ (16½, 17½, 19, 19)", ending with WS row.

- **Shape neck:** Work 21 (22, 22, 22, 23) sts, join 2nd ball of yarn and BO center 16 sts, cont across rem 21 (22, 22, 22, 23) sts. Working both sides at same time with separate balls of yarn, at beg of each neck edge, BO 3 sts once, dec 1 st EOR 2 (3, 3, 3, 4) times—16 sts each shoulder.

- Cont in patt until piece measures 19 (20, 21, 22½, 22½)". BO all sts.

FRONT

Work as for back.

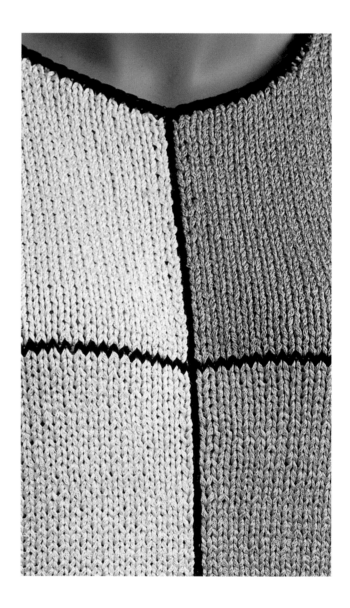

FINISHING

- **Black vertical chain on front and back:** Using crochet hook and 1 strand of A, with yarn underneath garment, insert hook into stitch between left and right colors on first row of A, wrap yarn around hook and pull loop through to RS (1 loop on hook). *Insert hook into next space above 2 strands of yarn of right-hand color, wrap yarn around hook and pull loop through to RS and through loop on hook (chain made). Rep from * to neck.

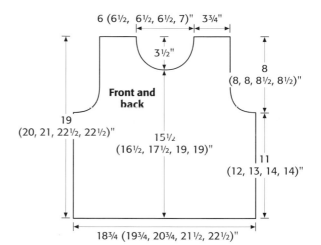

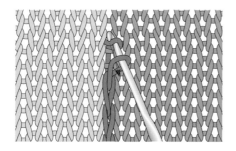

- Sew shoulder and side seams.
- **Neckband:** With RS of garment facing you, smaller needles, and A, PU 88 (92, 92, 92 96) sts evenly around neck edge. Join and BO all sts loosely.
- **Armbands:** With RS of garment facing you, smaller needles, and A, PU 74 (74, 76, 80, 80) sts evenly around armhole edge. Join and BO all sts loosely. Rep for 2nd armband.
- If necessary, block gently.

Yarn suggestion: String of Pearls from Muench (70% cotton, 20% rayon, 10% polyester; 50 g; 99 yds) in the following amounts and colors:

A	1 skein	color 4012
B	2 (2, 2, 3, 3) skeins	color 4014
C	2 (2, 2, 3, 3) skeins	color 4008
D	2 (2, 2, 3, 3) skeins	color 4004
E	2 (2, 2, 3, 3) skeins	color 4023

Dare-to-Wear Pink Shell

*When your wardrobe craves a little frill,
we dare you to wear this pink scoop neck with ruffle trim.
Go ahead, we double-dare you!*

Skill Level: Easy ◖■□◗
Sizes: Extra Small (Small, Medium, Large, Extra Large)
Finished Bust: 36 (37, 40, 42½, 44)"

Skill Builder

Picking up stitches on wrong side of fabric: Generally, picking up stitches is done on the right side of the garment. However, the unique design of the ruffled neck edge requires that the pickup be done on the wrong side to prevent the ridge from showing. With the wrong side of the work facing, insert the right-hand needle and knit the stitches onto the right-hand needle.

Melissa's Point

This one is just fabulous; I made it in three different colors. If you are not the ruffle type, make it without the ruffles and single crochet around all the edges.

DARE-TO-WEAR PINK SHELL

MATERIALS

3 (3, 3, 4, 4) skeins of Colinette Giotto (50% cotton, 40% rayon, 10% nylon; 100 g; 144 m), color 140 (**5**)

Size 10½ circular needles (24") or size required to obtain gauge

GAUGE

12 sts and 16 rows = 4" in St st

BACK

- CO 216 (224, 240, 256, 264) sts and work ruffle edge as follows:

    Row 1: K2tog across—108 (112 120, 128, 132) sts.

    Row 2: P2tog across—54 (56, 60, 64, 66) sts.

- Work in St st until piece measures 12½ (13½, 13½, 14½, 14½)", ending with WS row.

- **Shape armholes:** BO 4 sts at beg of next 2 rows. BO 2 sts at beg of next 2 rows. Dec 1 st at each edge EOR 2 (3, 4, 5, 6) times—38 (38, 40, 42, 42) sts.

- Cont in St st until piece measures 20 (21, 21, 22, 22)". BO all sts.

FRONT

- Work as for back until piece measures 13 (14, 14, 15, 15)", ending with WS row.

- **Cont with armhole shaping and AT SAME TIME shape neck:** Work across 17 (17, 18, 19, 19) sts, join 2nd ball of yarn and BO center 4 sts, work across rem 17 (17, 18, 19,

19) sts. Working both sides at same time with separate balls of yarn, at beg of each neck edge, BO 2 sts once, dec 1 st EOR 4 (4, 5, 5, 5) times—11 (11, 11, 12, 12) sts.

- Cont in St st until piece measures 20 (21, 21, 22, 22)". BO all sts.

FINISHING

- Sew shoulder and side seams.

- **Neck ruffle:** With WS facing, PU 68 (68, 72, 72, 72) sts evenly along neck edge and join.

Rnd 1: *K4, M1, rep from *—85 (85, 90, 90, 90) sts.

Rnd 2 and all even rnds: Knit.

Rnd 3: *K4, M1, rep from * to last 1 (1, 2, 2, 2) sts, knit to end—106 (106, 112, 112, 112) sts.

Rnd 5: *K4, M1, rep from * to last 2 (2, 0, 0, 0) sts, knit to end—132 (132, 140, 140, 140) sts.

Rnd 7: *K4, M1, rep from *—165 (165, 175, 175, 175) sts.

Rnd 9: *K1, M1, rep from *—330 (330, 350, 350, 350) sts.

Rnd 11: *K1, M1, rep from *—660 (660, 700, 700, 700) sts.

Rnd 13: K1f&b around—1320 (1320, 1400, 1400, 1400) sts. BO all sts.

- If necessary, block gently.

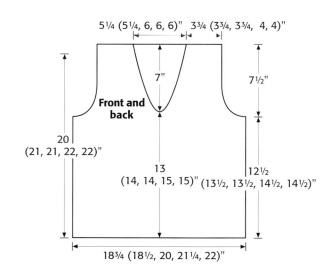

5¼ (5¼, 6, 6, 6)" 3¾ (3¾, 3¾, 4, 4)"

7"

7½"

Front and back

20 (21, 21, 22, 22)"

13 (14, 14, 15, 15)" 12½ (13½, 13½, 14½, 14½)"

18¾ (18½, 20, 21¼, 22)"

Red tank: 6 (7, 7, 8, 9) skeins of Tartelette from Knit One Crochet Too (50% cotton, 40% Tactel nylon, 10% nylon: 50g; 75 yds), color 260.

Cream tank: 5 (6, 6, 7, 8) skeins of Venecia from Katia (53% polyamide, 37% viscose, 10% nylon; 50 g; 85 yds), color 3204. Only 6 rows of neck finishing were worked for fewer ruffles.

Feather Shell

The nicely textured Farrow Rib pattern provides a shapely, yet comfortable fit. The applied feather yoke turns this tank into a fashion statement.

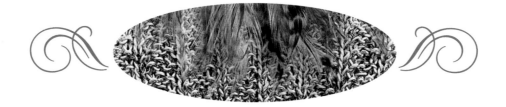

Skill Level: Easy ◧▪▢▢

Sizes: Extra Small (Small, Medium, Large, Extra Large)
Finished Bust: 38½ (40½, 42½, 44½, 46½)"

Skill Builder

Applying purchased trim: Using a sewing needle and matching thread, baste trim in place on the right side of the neck edge. Fold neckband forward over the trim and baste in place. Final stitching can be done either by hand with a sewing needle and thread or with a sewing machine.

Melissa's Point

I'm still waiting for a date to wear this—or I mean second date; it's probably not appropriate for a first date. In the meantime, I will just wear it to the shop.

FEATHER SHELL

MATERIALS

A 4 (4, 4, 5, 5) skeins of Millefili Fine from Filatura di Crosa (100% cotton; 50 g; 136 yds), color 128 ③

B 3 (3, 3, 4, 4) skeins of Pixel from Filatura di Crosa (80% viscose, 20% polyamide; 50 g; 176 yds), color 4 ②

1 yard of feather trim or other purchased novelty trim

Size 8 circular needles (24") or size required to obtain gauge

Size 11 needles (for neck BO only)

Sewing needle and matching thread

GAUGE

16 sts and 20 rows = 4" in Farrow Rib patt (slightly stretched) on smaller needles with 1 strand each of A and B held tog

FARROW RIB PATTERN
(Multiple of 4 + 1)

All rows: *K3, P1, rep from * to last st, K1.

BACK

- With smaller needles and 1 strand each of A and B held tog, CO 77 (81, 85, 89, 93) sts and work in Farrow Rib patt until piece measures 13 (13, 14, 14, 15)", ending with WS row.

- **Shape armholes:** BO 5 (5, 6, 6, 7) sts at beg of next 2 rows, dec 1 st at each edge EOR 4 (4, 5, 6, 6) times—59 (63, 63, 65, 67) sts. Cont in patt until piece measures 15 (15, 16, 16, 17)", ending with RS row.

- **Shape neck:** Work across 25 (27, 27, 28, 29) sts, join 2nd ball of yarn and BO center 9 (9, 9, 9, 9) sts, work across rem 25 (27, 27, 28, 29) sts. Working both sides at same time with separate balls of yarn, at beg of each neck edge, BO 3 sts once, dec 1 st EOR 6 (7, 7, 8, 9) times—16 (17, 17, 17, 17) sts.

- Cont in patt until piece measures 21 (21, 22, 22, 23)". BO in patt.

FRONT

Work as for back.

FINISHING

- Sew shoulder and side seams.

- **Neckband:** With smaller needles and RS facing, beg at right shoulder, PU 88 (88, 88, 92, 92) sts evenly around neck edge. Join and work in K1, P1 ribbing for 1". With larger needles, BO in patt very loosely. With sewing needle and matching thread, baste feather trim 2" down from neck edge on RS. Tack neck-edge rib over feather trim on RS and sew in place.

- Block only if you want to relax the ribbing.

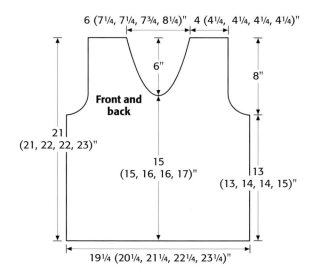

6 (7¼, 7¼, 7¾, 8¼)" 4 (4¼, 4¼, 4¼, 4¼)"

6"

Front and back

8"

21 (21, 22, 22, 23)"

15 (15, 16, 16, 17)"

13 (13, 14, 14, 15)"

19¼ (20¼, 21¼, 22¼, 23¼)"

Black feather shell: 5 (6, 6, 7, 7) skeins of String of Pearls from Muench (70% cotton, 20% viscose, 10% polyester; 50 g; 99 yds), color 4012, Black

Lace Halter

The center lace panel transforms a basic halter into a flattering and airy option—ideal for balmy conditions.

Skill Level: Intermediate ◼◼◼◻

Sizes: Extra Small (Small, Medium, Large, Extra Large)

Finished Bust: 33½ (37, 40½, 44, 47½)"

Skill Builder

ssk (slip slip knit): Slip two stitches onto the right needle, one at a time, as if to knit. Insert the point of the left needle into the front of the two slipped stitches; knit the stitches together through the back of the loops. This produces a left-slanting decrease.

Melissa's Point

This is a great piece for your summer wardrobe. Halter bras are available and recommended for those over 40.

LACE HALTER

MATERIALS

A 3 (4, 4, 5, 5) skeins of Fixation from Cascade Yarns (98.3% cotton, 1.7% elastic; 50 g; 100 yds), color 8176 ⓸

B 3 (4, 4, 5, 5) skeins of String of Pearls from Muench Yarns (70% cotton, 20% viscose, 10% polyester; 50 g; 99 yds), color 4011 ⓸

Size 10 needles or size required to obtain gauge

Size J crochet hook

2 ring markers

GAUGE

14 sts and 18 rows = 4" in St st with one strand each of A and B held tog

LACE PATTERN
(Multiple of 11)

Row 1 (RS): K4, K2tog, YO, K5.

Row 2 and all WS rows: Purl.

Row 3: K3, K2tog, YO, K1, YO, ssk, K3.

Alternative yarn: 6 (7, 7, 8, 8) skeins of Rondo from S. Charles (55% cotton, 35% viscose, 10% polyamide; 50 g; 88 yds). Use only 1 strand of Rondo for this garment.

Row 5: K2, K2tog, YO, K3, YO, ssk, K2.

Row 7: K1, K2tog, YO, K5, YO, ssk, K1.

Row 9: K2tog, YO, K2, K2tog, YO, K3, YO, ssk.

Row 10: Purl.

Rep rows 3–10 for patt.

BACK

With 1 strand each of A and B held tog, CO 59 (65, 71, 77, 83) sts and work in St st until piece measures 10 (12, 14, 15, 15)". BO all sts.

The halter back is high enough to hide a strapless bra.

FRONT

- With 1 strand each of A and B held tog, CO 59 (65, 71, 77, 83) sts and work 24 (27, 30, 33, 36) sts in St st, pm, work 11 sts in lace patt, pm, work rem 24 (27, 30, 33, 36) sts in St st. Cont in patt until piece measures 10 (12, 14, 15, 15)", ending with WS row.

- **Shape armholes:** BO 4 sts at beg of next 2 rows. Dec 1 st at each edge EOR 10 (10, 11, 11, 12) times.

- **AT SAME TIME when piece measures 11 (13, 15, 16, 16)", ending with row 10, shape neck:** Work across to center 3 sts, BO center 3 sts, work across rem sts. Working both sides at same time with separate balls of yarn, at each neck edge, dec 1 st EOR 10 (10, 11, 11, 12) times—4 (5, 5, 6, 6) sts each shoulder.

- Cont in St st until piece measures 20 (22, 24, 25½, 25½)". Shoulder straps of 2½", which will meet at center back neck, are included in this measurement. BO all sts.

FINISHING

- Sew side seams.

- Weave shoulder-strap ends tog at back of neck.

- **Neck and armhole edges:** With 1 strand each of A and B held tog and RS facing, work 1 row of sc around neck edge and each armhole edge.

- If necessary, block gently.

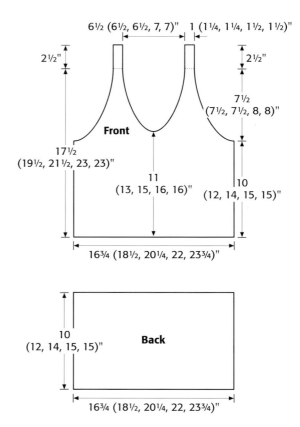

Venus Shell

With a refined wear-with-anything versatility, this tank is smart and stylish. The uneven edge is accented with the pattern stitch.

Skill Level: Easy ■■□□

Sizes: Extra Small (Small, Medium, Large, Extra Large)

Finished Bust: 31½ (36½, 41½, 46½, 51½)"

Skill Builder

Shrimp stitch: Work a foundation row of single crochet. Without turning, work a row of single crochet in reverse. Work left to right, inserting the hook into the stitch to the right and complete the single crochet.

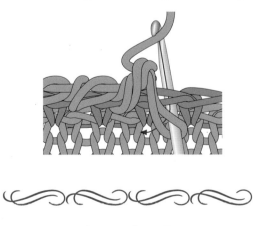

Melissa's Point

This is a slimming and attractive wardrobe addition. It looks great in every size.

VENUS SHELL

MATERIALS

5, (6, 8, 9, 10) skeins of Venus from S. Charles (95% viscose, 5% polyamide; 50 g; 81 yds), color 22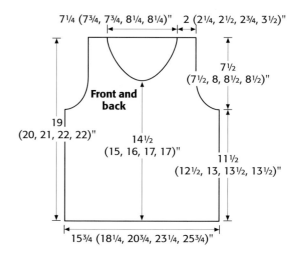

Size 8 needles or size required to obtain gauge

Size F crochet hook

GAUGE

16 sts and 20 rows = 4" in St st

CHEVRON PATTERN
(Multiple of 10 + 13)

VDD (Vertical Double Decrease): Insert right needle into 2 sts at the same time as if to knit, slip to right needle, knit next st, pass both slipped sts over knit st and off right needle.

Row 1 (RS): K1, K2tog, K3, *YO, K1, YO, K3, VDD, K3, rep from * to last 7 sts, YO, K1, YO, K3, ssk, K1.

Row 2: Purl.

Rep rows 1 and 2.

BACK

- CO 63 (73, 83, 93, 103) sts and work in Chevron patt until piece measures 7" ending with WS row.

- Change to St st and work until piece measures 11½ (12½, 13, 13½, 13½)", ending with WS row.

- **Shape armholes:** BO 3 (4, 5, 6, 7) sts at beg of next 2 rows. BO 2 (3, 4, 4, 5) sts at beg of next 2 rows. Dec 1 st at each edge EOR 4 (5, 7, 9, 9) times—45 (49, 51, 55, 61) sts.

- Cont in patt until piece measures 19 (20, 21, 22, 22)". BO all sts.

FRONT

- Work as for back until piece measures 14½ (15, 16, 17, 17)", ending with WS row.

- **Shape neck:** Work across 13 (15, 16, 18, 21) sts, join 2nd ball of yarn and BO center 19 sts, work across rem 13 (15, 16, 18, 21) sts. Working both sides at same time with separate balls of yarn, at beg of each neck edge, BO 3 sts once, BO 2 sts once, dec 1 st 0 (1, 1, 2, 2) times—8 (9, 10, 11, 14) sts each shoulder.

- Cont in patt until piece measures 19 (20, 21, 22, 22)". BO all sts.

FINISHING

- Sew shoulder and side seams.

- **Neck and armhole edges:** With RS facing, work 1 row of sc followed by 1 row of shrimp st (see Skill Builder) around neck and armhole edges.

- If necessary, block gently.

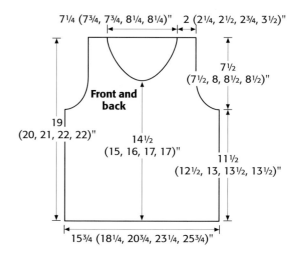

7¼ (7¾, 7¾, 8¼, 8¼)" 2 (2¼, 2½, 2¾, 3½)"

7½ (7½, 8, 8½, 8½)"

Front and back

19 (20, 21, 22, 22)"

14½ (15, 16, 17, 17)"

11½ (12½, 13, 13½, 13½)"

15¾ (18¼, 20¾, 23¼, 25¾)"

Create a smart twin set by pairing this shell with a black version of the Seventies with Taste cardigan on page 86. For cardigan only, you will need the following amounts:

A 16 (17, 18) skeins of Victoria from S Charles (60% cotton, 40% viscose; 50 g; 70 yds), color 12

B 1 skein of Venus from S Charles (95% viscose, 5% polyamide; 50 g; 81 yds), color 22

Big Vest

*The details—the button placket and wide collar—
separate this big vest from all the rest.*

Skill Level: Easy ◖■□◻

Sizes: Extra Small (Small, Medium, Large, Extra Large)

Finished Bust: 38 (40, 42, 44, 46)"

Skill Builder

Seaming: For less bulky seams, use a lighter-weight yarn with the same
color and fiber content as the project yarn to sew the seams.

Melissa's Point

This vest is so easy. The buttons are just for looks,
so you don't even need to make buttonholes.

BIG VEST

MATERIALS

4 (5, 5, 6, 7) skeins of Big Wool from Rowan (100% merino wool; 100 g; 80 m), color 022 (6)

Size 15 needles or size required to obtain gauge

Size 13 circular needles (24")

Small amount of lightweight yarn in matching color for seams

3 buttons, ⅞" diameter

GAUGE

8 sts and 12 rows = 4" in St st on larger needles

BACK

- With smaller needles, CO 38 (40, 42, 44, 46) sts. Work in K2, P2 ribbing for 2" ending with WS row.
- Change to larger needles and work in St st until piece measures 11 (12, 13, 13, 14)", ending with WS row.
- **Shape armhole:** BO 3 sts at beg of next 2 rows. Dec 1 st at each edge EOR 3 (3, 3, 3, 4) times— 26 (28, 30, 32, 32) sts.
- Cont in St st until piece measures 20 (21, 22, 22, 23)". BO all sts loosely.

FRONT

- Work as for back until piece measures 8 (9, 10, 10, 11)", ending with WS row.
- **Shape placket:** Work 17 (18, 19, 20, 21) sts, join 2nd ball of yarn and BO center 4 sts, cont in patt across 17 (18, 19, 20, 21) sts. Working both sides at same time with separate balls of yarn, cont in St st until piece measures 11 (12, 13, 13, 14)", ending with WS row.
- **Shape armholes:** BO 3 sts at beg of next 2 rows. Dec 1 st at each edge EOR 3 (3, 3, 3, 4) times—11 (12, 13, 14, 14) sts each side. Cont in patt until piece measures 13 (14, 15, 15, 16)", ending with WS row.

- **Shape neck:** Dec 1 st at each neck edge EOR 7 (7, 7, 8, 8) times as follows: For left side, knit to last 3 sts, K2tog, K1; for right side, K1, sl 1, K1, ssk, knit to end—4 (5, 6, 6, 6) sts each shoulder.
- Cont in St st until piece measures 20 (21, 22, 22, 23)". BO loosely.

FINISHING

- Sew shoulder seams with lightweight yarn.
- **Placket and neck:** With smaller needles and RS facing, beg at bottom of placket, PU 18 sts along placket edge, 24 sts along right neck, 14 (14, 14, 18, 18) sts along back, 24 sts along left neck, 18 sts along placket—98 (98, 98, 102, 102) sts. Do not join; work in K2, P2 ribbing for 1¼" ending with WS row. BO 18 sts (placket sts) at beg of next 2 rows.
- **Collar:** Cont in St st until collar is 5". BO all sts in patt.
- **Armhole edges:** With smaller needles and RS facing, PU 52 sts along armhole edge. Join and work in K2, P2 ribbing for 1¼" ending with WS row. BO loosely in patt. Rep for 2nd armhole.
- Sew side seams with lightweight yarn.
- If necessary, block gently.
- Sew on buttons.

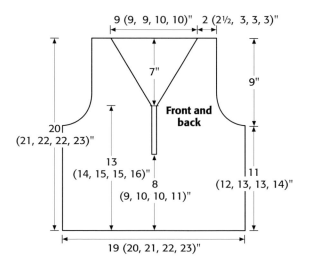

9 (9, 9, 10, 10)" 2 (2½, 3, 3, 3)"

7"

9"

Front and back

20 (21, 22, 22, 23)"

13 (14, 15, 15, 16)"

8 (9, 10, 10, 11)"

11 (12, 13, 13, 14)"

19 (20, 21, 22, 23)"

A BIT ON BUTTONS

Buttons are much more than basic fasteners for closing garments. Used as an embellishment, buttons decorate and add style. The right button can finish off a garment perfectly. Here are a few things to consider when selecting that perfect button.

There are two basic types of buttons: shank buttons and flat sew-through buttons with either two or four holes. Shank buttons have a solid top and a shank or spacer that raises the button from the knit fabric. Flat buttons are fine for nonfunctioning, decorative applications. Shank buttons are best for heavier knit fabrics.

The color of the button can be a perfect match or a contrasting or complementary color, depending on whether you want the button to blend in with the garment or distinctly stand out. A button with texture may harmonize with the knit fabric, but choose a button without rough edges that may catch on the yarn. For an unexpected look, consider mismatched buttons. For a fun and appealing look, select novelty buttons.

Proportion is key when choosing button size. Generally, smaller buttons give a more delicate look, and more buttons are applied. Consider lightweight buttons for knits of lighter weight. Heavy buttons may pull and distort the knit fabric. A heavier bulky knit fabric requires a larger, more substantial button(s). The larger the button, the fewer buttons required.

Select a sewing needle with an eye small enough to go through the button and large enough to thread the yarn through. Craft or large-eye hand needles in sizes 18–22 usually work best. If the knitting yarn is bulky, select a thinner, smooth yarn in a comparable color. Use a needle threader to thread the yarn through the eye of the needle.

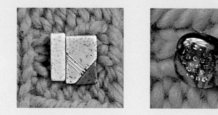

Diagonal Suede Vest

Create a little western chic with this diagonal-stitch vest trimmed with long, flowing fringe.

Skill Level: Easy ◼◼☐▷

Sizes: Small (Medium, Large)

Finished Bust: 34 (38, 46)"

Skill Builder

Make 1 (M1): Make a stitch by inserting the left needle from front to back under the horizontal strand between the two stitches. Knit this lifted strand through the back loop.

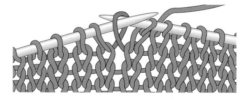

Melissa's Point

Yee-haw! I never thought of myself as the cowgirl type, but this vest changed all that. I may have to add cowboy boots to my shoe collection.

DIAGONAL SUEDE VEST

MATERIALS

4 (5, 6) skeins of Suede from Berroco (100% nylon; 50 g; 120 yds), color Maverick 3716

Size 9 needles or size required to obtain gauge

Size I crochet hook

2 ring markers

1 button, 1¾" diameter, with shank

GAUGE

18 sts and 21 rows = 4" in St st

BACK

- CO 92 (98, 106) sts and work setup row: K45 (48, 52), pm, K2, pm, K45 (48, 52).

- Work back diagonal patt as follows:

  Row 1 and all WS rows: Purl.

  Row 2: K1, M1, knit to 2 sts before marker, ssk, sl marker, K2, sl marker, K2tog, knit to last st, M1, K1.

  Rep rows 1 and 2 until piece measures 2½ (3, 3½)" at side edge, ending with WS row.

- **Shape armholes:**

  Next row (RS): BO 5 (7, 8) sts at side edge, knit to 2 sts before marker, ssk, sl marker, K2, sl marker, K2tog, knit to end.

  Next row: BO 5 (7, 8) sts at side edge, purl across.

  Next row: Knit to 2 sts before marker, ssk, sl marker, K2, sl marker, K2tog, knit to end.

  Next row: Purl across.

  Rep last 2 rows 2 more times—74 (76, 82) sts at end of armhole shaping.

- Cont to work rows 1 and 2 of back diagonal patt as above until armhole measures 8 (9, 10)", ending with WS row.

- **Shape shoulders:**

  Next row (RS): BO 2 sts at armhole edge, knit to 2 sts before marker, ssk, sl marker, K2, sl marker, K2tog, knit to end.

  Next row: BO 2 sts at armhole edge, purl across.

  Rep last 2 rows 10 (10, 11) more times. BO rem 8 (10, 10) sts.

LEFT FRONT

- CO 46 (49, 53) sts and work left diagonal patt as follows:

  Row 1 (RS): K1, M1, knit to last 3 sts, ssk, K1.

  Row 2 and all WS rows: Purl.

  Rep rows 1 and 2 until piece measures 2½ (3, 3½)" at side edge, ending with WS row.

DIAGONAL SUEDE VEST

- **Shape armhole and neck:** Work armhole and neck shaping at same time as follows:

  Next row (RS): BO 5 (7, 8) sts at armhole edge, knit to last 4 sts, sl 2, K2tog, psso, K1.

  Next row: Purl across.

  Next row: Knit to last 5 sts, sl 2, K2tog, p2sso, K1.

  Next row: Purl across.

  Rep last 2 rows 1 more time—32 (33, 36) sts.

- **Cont neck shaping:**

  Next row (RS): Knit to last 4 sts, sl 1, K2tog, psso, K1.

  Next row: Purl across.

  Rep last 2 rows 4 more times—22 (23, 26) sts at end of armhole and neck shaping.

- Cont to work rows 1 and 2 of left diagonal patt as on page 34 until armhole measures 8 (9, 10)", ending with WS row.

- **Shape shoulder:**

  Next row (RS): BO 2 sts at armhole edge, knit to last 3 sts, ssk, K1.

  Next row: Purl across.

  Rep last 2 rows 5 (5, 6) more times. BO rem 4 (5, 5) sts.

RIGHT FRONT

- CO 46 (49, 53) sts and work right diagonal patt as follows:

  Row 1 and all WS rows: Purl.

  Row 2 (RS): K1, K2tog, knit to last st, M1, K1.

  Rep rows 1 and 2 until piece measures 2½ (3, 3½)" at side edge, ending with RS row.

- **Shape armhole and neck:** Work armhole and neck shaping at same time as follows:

  Next row (WS): BO 5 (7, 8) sts at armhole edge, purl to end.

  Next row: K1, K4tog, knit to end.

  Next row: Purl across.

  Next row: K1, K4tog, knit to end.

  Rep last 2 rows 1 more time—32 (33, 36) sts.

- **Cont neck shaping:**

  Next row (WS): Purl across.

  Next row: K1, K3tog, knit to end.

  Rep last 2 rows 4 more times—22 (23, 26) sts at end of armhole and neck shaping.

- Cont to work rows 1 and 2 of right diagonal patt as for right front until armhole measures 8 (9, 10)", ending with RS row.

- **Shape shoulder:**

  Next row (WS): BO 2 sts at armhole edge, purl to end.

  Next row: K1, K2tog, knit to end.

  Rep last 2 rows 5 (5, 6) more times. BO rem 4 (5, 5) sts.

FINISHING

- Sew shoulders and side seams.

- **Neck and armhole edges:** With RS facing, work 1 row of sc along neck and armhole edges.

- **Fringe:** Cut enough 20" lengths of fringe to go around bottom of front and back. Attach 2 strands of fringe in approx every 3rd st along bottom edges of front and back (see page 100).

- Sew on button. Attach single strand of fringe opposite the button and wrap around button shank to close.

- Do not block.

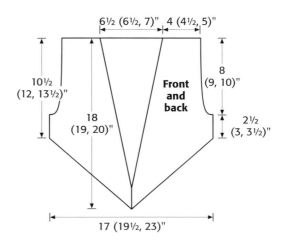

Woven-Look Vest

Show your passion for color and texture. Receive a standing ovation for your elegant and refined style.

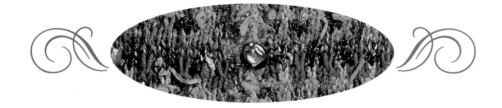

Skill Level: Easy ◖■☐▷

Sizes: Extra Small (Small, Medium, Large, Extra Large)

Finished Bust: 37¾ (38¾, 41¾, 45½, 49½)"

Skill Builder

Slipping stitches: Slip stitches as if to purl unless the pattern indicates otherwise. Slip stitches with yarn in back (wyib) on right-side rows, and with yarn in front (wyif) on wrong-side rows. When shaping, omit the slip stich if it occurs on an edge. Instead, work the edge stitch with the yarn used in the row.

Melissa's Point

If you are color shy, don't panic. For a striking combination, pick out six yarns with different textures and colors. Throw together in a basket and see how well they work.

WOVEN-LOOK VEST

MATERIALS

A 2 (2, 2, 2, 3,) skeins of Cleo from Muench Yarns (63% rayon, 16% wool, 14% metal, 7% nylon; 50 g; 62 yds), color 143 **④**

B 1 (1, 1, 2, 2) skeins of All Season Cotton from Rowan (60% cotton, 40% acrylic; 50 g; 90 m), color 214 **④**

C 1 (1, 1, 2, 2) skeins of String of Pearls from Muench Yarns (70% cotton, 20% rayon, 10% polyester; 50 g; 99 yds), color 4009 **④**

D 2 (2, 2, 3, 3) skeins of Siam from Trendsetter Yarns (60% cotton, 40% polyamide; 50 g ; 110 yds), color 5777 **④**

E 1 (1, 1, 2, 2) skeins of Ritratto from S. Charles (50% rayon, 30% kid mohair, 10% nylon, 10% polyester; 50 g; 198 yds), color 72 **③**

F 1 (1, 1, 2, 2) skeins of Aquarius from Trendsetter (78% nylon, 22% cotton; 50 g; 96 yds), color 819 **④**

Size 8 needles or size required to obtain gauge

Size G crochet hook

7 glass buttons, ½" diameter

GAUGE

17 sts and 21 rows = 4" in Woven patt st after blocking

WOVEN PATTERN STITCH
(Multiple of 4 + 2)

Row 1 (RS): K1, *K3, sl 1 wyib, rep from * to last st, K1.

Row 2: Purl the purl sts and sl the slipped sts wyif.

Row 3: K1, *K1, sl 1 wyib, K2, rep from * to last st, K1.

Row 4: Purl the purl sts and sl the slipped sts wyif.

Rep rows 1–4, following color sequence.

COLOR SEQUENCE

2 rows with B

2 rows with A

2 rows with E, worked with 2 strands held tog

2 rows with C

2 rows with F

2 rows with D

Rep for color sequence.

BACK

- With 2 strands of E held tog, CO 78 (82, 96, 94, 102) sts and beg Woven patt st, following color sequence. Work until piece measures 10 (12, 13, 14, 15)", ending with WS row.

- **Shape armholes:** BO 4 sts at beg of next 2 rows, dec 1 st at each edge EOR 2 (2, 3, 3, 4) times—66 (70, 72, 80, 86) sts.

- Cont in patt until piece measures 20 (22, 23, 24, 26)". BO all sts.

LEFT FRONT

- With 2 strands of E held tog, CO 42 (42, 46, 50, 54) sts and beg Woven patt st, following color sequence. Work until piece measures 10 (12, 13, 14, 15)", ending with WS row.

- **Shape armhole and neck:** For armhole, BO 4 sts at side edge once, dec 1 st at side edge EOR 2 (2, 3, 3, 4) times. AT SAME TIME for neck, work to last 3 sts, K2tog, K1 at neck edge every 4 rows 13 (13, 16, 16, 16) times. Cont in patt on 23 (23, 23, 27, 30) sts each shoulder until piece measures 20 (22, 23, 24, 26)". BO rem sts.

RIGHT FRONT

- Work as for left front, reversing shaping. **Neck dec:** K1, sl 1, K1, psso, knit to end.

FINISHING

- Sew shoulder, sleeve, and side seams.

- Place marker for 7 buttonholes along right side.

- **Neck, front, and bottom edges:** With RS facing and D, beg at right shoulder, work 1 row of sc along neck, front, and bottom edges. Ch 1 for buttonhole at markers.

- **Armhole edges:** With RS facing and D, beg at underarm seam, work 1 row of sc along each armhole edge.

- Block gently.

- Sew on buttons.

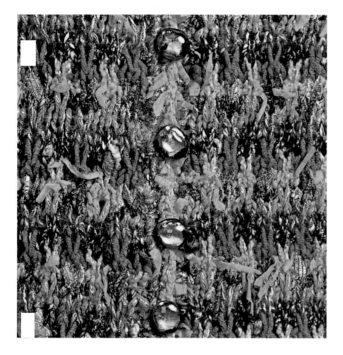

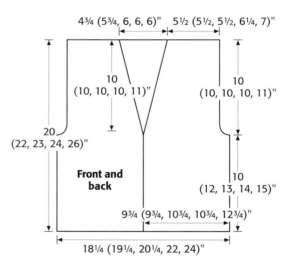

Colored Ladders V-Neck

Take a classic V-neck, add colored ladders, and you have a contemporary pullover with long, slimming lines.

Skill Level: Intermediate ⬛⬛⬛▢

Sizes: Extra Small (Small, Medium, Large, Extra Large)

Finished Bust: 34½ (37, 40, 42½, 45)"

Skill Builder

Selecting colors: Choose contrasting colors of yarn for this project.
The full effect of the pattern stitch will be lost if the two colors are too similar.

Melissa's Point

This stitch pattern looks more complicated than it really is. After the first few repeats, it's a perfect TV project and does not require your constant attention.

COLORED LADDERS V-NECK

MATERIALS

A 2 (2, 2, 3, 3) skeins of Clip from Klaus Koch Kollection (100% cotton; 100 g; 183 yds) color 05

B 1 hank of Laurel from Schafer Yarn Company (100% cotton; 8 oz; 400 yds) color hand dyed

Size 9 needles or size required to obtain gauge

Size 7 circular needles (24)"

GAUGE

19 sts and 22 rows = 4" in Ladder st on larger needles after blocking

LADDER STITCH
(Multiple of 6 + 5)

Row 1 (RS): With A, K2, sl 1 wyib, *K5, sl 1, rep from * to last 2 sts, K2.

Row 2: With A, P2, sl 1 wyif, *P5, slip 1, rep from * to last 2 sts, P2.

Row 3: With B, K5, *sl 1 wyib, K5, rep from *.

Row 4: With B, K5, *sl 1 wyif, K5, rep from *.

Rep rows 1–4.

BACK

- With A and smaller needles, CO 83 (89, 95, 101, 107) sts. With B, knit 2 rows; with A, knit 2 rows; with B, knit 2 rows.

- Change to A and larger needles, work in Ladder st until piece measures 12½ (12½, 13, 14, 14½)", ending with WS row.

- **Shape armholes:** BO 5 sts at beg of next 2 rows. Dec 1 st at each edge EOR 7 times—59 (65, 71, 77, 83) sts.

- Cont in patt until piece measures 20 (20, 21, 22, 23)". BO all sts.

FRONT

- Work as for back until piece measures 15 (15, 16, 17, 18)", ending with row 2 of Ladder st.

- **Shape neck:** Work in patt across 29 (32, 35, 38, 41) sts, join 2nd ball of yarn and BO center st, cont in pattern across rem 29 (32, 35, 38, 41) sts. Working both sides at same time with separate balls of yarn, dec 1 st at each neck edge EOR 16 times—13 (16, 19, 22, 25) sts.

- Cont in patt until piece measures 20 (20, 21, 22, 23)". BO all sts.

SLEEVES

- With A and smaller needles, CO 59 (59, 65, 65, 71) sts. With B, knit 2 rows; with A, knit 2 rows; with B, knit 2 rows.

- Change to A and larger needles, work in Ladder st, inc 1 st at each edge every 4 rows 2 times—63 (63, 69, 69, 75) sts. Cont in patt until piece measures 3½" ending with WS row.

- **Shape cap:** BO 5 sts at beg of next 2 rows. Dec 1 st at each edge EOR 14 (14, 16, 16, 16) times. BO 3 sts at beg of next 4 rows—13 (13, 15, 15, 21) sts. BO rem sts.

FINISHING

- Sew shoulder seams.

- **Neck edge:** With RS facing, beg at right shoulder with A and smaller needles, PU 37 sts along back, 34 sts along left front, center st, 34 sts along right front—106 sts. Join and knit to 2 sts from center front, ssk, knit center st, K2tog, knit to end. Purl 1 rnd. BO all sts.

- Sew sleeve and side seams.

- If necessary, block gently.

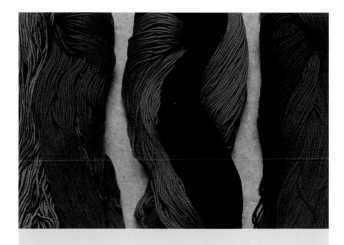

Colors	Colors	Colors
169 and 165	146 and 24	146 and 20

For a bolder look, pair two solid colors.

Yarn suggestions: Clip from Klaus Koch Kollection (100% cotton; 100 g; 183 yds) in the following amounts:

A 2 (2, 2, 3, 3) skeins

B 2 (2, 2, 3, 3) skeins

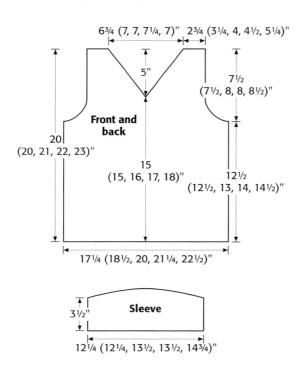

Claws and Ribs Pullover

This tunic is irresistibly comfortable.
The simple long lines, textured claw cable and rib pattern,
and funnel neck supply the distinguishing
features to this oversized tunic.

Skill Level: Intermediate ■■■□
Sizes: Extra Small (Small, Medium, Large, Extra Large)
Finished Bust: 40½ (45, 49, 53½, 57½)"

Skill Builder

Allowing ease: Ease is the amount of extra fabric beyond body
measurements. Ease ensures a comfortable fit. An oversized sweater should be
at least 6" to 10" larger than actual body measurements.

Melissa's Point

This looks wonderful over a long, slim skirt and just as good over jeans.
A great sweater for lounging by the fireplace—if only I had a fireplace.

CLAWS AND RIBS PULLOVER

MATERIALS

14 (15, 16, 17, 19) skeins of Cashmerino from Debbie Bliss (55% merino wool, 33% microfiber, 12% cashmere; 50 g; 90 m), color 103 (4)

Size 8 needles or size required to obtain gauge

Size 7 circular needles (24")

Cable needle

2 stitch holders

2 ring markers

GAUGE

19 sts and 25 rows = 4" in St st on larger needles

CABLE ABBREVIATIONS

C4R (Cross 4 Right): Sl 3 sts onto cn and hold in back, K1, K3 from cn.

C4L (Cross 4 Left): Sl 1 st onto cn and hold in front, K3, K1 from cn.

BACK

- With smaller needles, CO 97 (107, 117, 127, 137) sts and beg ribbing patt as follows:

  Row 1 (RS): (P1, K1tbl) twice, P1, K2tog, YO, K1, K4, (K3, P2) 5 (6, 7, 8, 9) times, K1, K2tog, YO, K1, K4, (P1, K1tbl) 3 times, P1, K4, K1, YO, ssk, K1, (P2, K3) 5 (6, 7, 8, 9) times, K4, K1, YO, ssk, (P1, K1tbl) twice, P1.

  Rows 2 and 4: Knit the knit sts and purl the YO and purl sts.

  Row 3: (P1, K1tbl) twice, P1, K2tog, YO, K1, C4R, (K3, P2) 5 (6, 7, 8, 9) times, K1, K2tog, YO, K1, C4L, (P1, K1tbl) 3 times, P1, C4R, K1, YO, ssk, K1, (P2, K3) 5 (6, 7, 8, 9) times, C4L, K1, YO, ssk, (P1, K1tbl) twice, P1.

  Rep rows 1–4 until piece measures 2½", ending with WS row.

- Change to larger needles and beg Claw and Rib patt as follows:

  Row 1 (RS): (P1, K1tbl) twice, P1, K2tog, YO, K1, K4, K25 (30, 35, 40, 45), K1, K2 tog, YO, K1, K4, (P1, K1tbl) 3 times, P1, K4, K1, YO, ssk, K1, K25 (30, 35, 40, 45), K4, K1, YO, ssk, (P1, K1tbl) twice, P1.

  Rows 2 and 4: Knit the knit sts and purl the YO and purl sts.

  Row 3: (P1, K1tbl) twice, P1, K2tog, YO, K1, C4R, K25 (30, 35, 40, 45), K1, K2tog, YO, K1, C4L, (P1, K1tbl) 3 times, P1, C4R, K1, YO, ssk, K1, K25 (30, 35, 40, 45), C4L, K1, YO, ssk, (P1, K1tbl) twice, P1.

  Rep rows 1–4 until piece measures 22 (24, 25, 26, 27)".

- **Shoulders and neck:** BO 26 (31, 36, 41, 46) sts at beg of next 2 rows. Place center 45 sts on st holder for neck.

FRONT

Work as for back.

SLEEVES

- With smaller needles, CO 45 (45, 55, 55, 55) sts and work ribbing patt as follows:

  Row 1 (RS): (P2, K3) 2 (3) times, P2, K1, K2tog, YO, K1, K4, (P1, K1tbl) 3 times, P1, K4, K1, YO, ssk, K1, (P2, K3) 2 (3) times.

  Rows 2 and 4: Knit the knit sts and purl the YO and purl sts.

  Row 3: (P2, K3) 2 (3) times, P2, K1, K2tog, YO, K1, C4L, (P1, K1tbl) 3 times, P1, C4R, K1, YO, ssk, K1, (P2, K3) 2 (3) times.

  Rep rows 1–4 until piece measures 2½", ending with WS row.

- Change to larger needles and rep rows 1–4, inc 1 st at each edge every 4 rows 14 (14, 14, 16, 16) times—73 (73, 83, 87, 87) sts.

- Cont in patt until piece measures 15". BO all sts.

FINISHING

- Sew shoulder seams.

- **Collar:** With smaller needles, work neck sts from holders, pm at each shoulder seam. Join and knit around, maintaining patt on 23 center sts as follows:

  Rnd 1 (RS): K1, K2tog, YO, K1, K4, (P1, K1tbl) 3 times, P1, K4, K1, YO, ssk, K1. Dec 1 st at each shoulder after marker every 4 rows 3 times.

  Rnds 2 and 4: Knit the knit sts and purl the YO and purl sts.

  Rnd 3: K1, K2tog, YO, K1, C4L, (P1, K1tbl) 3 times, P1, C4R, K1, YO, ssk, K1.

  Rep rnds 1–4, dec 1 st at each shoulder after marker every 4 rnds 3 times. Cont in patt and inc 1 st at each shoulder after marker every 4 rnds 3 times.

  Cont in patt until collar measures 5". Knit all sts for 2". BO all sts loosely. Fold collar in half inward and tack on inside.

- Sew sleeve and side seams, leaving bottom 6" open for side slits.

- If necessary, block gently.

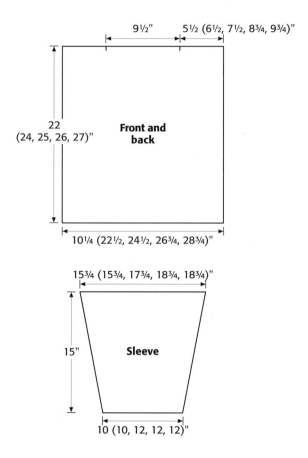

DNA Pullover

James Watson and Francis Crick published their report proposing the structure of DNA in 1953. Today, this double helix is widely recognized. Impress others, bask in their compliments, and enjoy the comfortable fit.

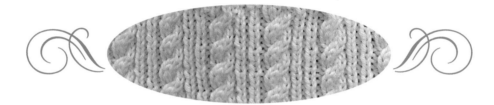

Skill Level: Intermediate ◼◼◼◻

Sizes: Extra Small (Small, Medium, Large, Extra Large)

Finished Bust: 34½ (38, 42½, 46, 50½)"

Skill Builder

Using ring markers: Place ring markers between cable patterns if desired. Move markers by slipping from the left to the right needle.

Melissa's Point

This is the one to knit if you are single. Wear it, and when that handsome gentleman recognizes the pattern, snag him—he is an educated man.

DNA PULLOVER

MATERIALS

11 (12, 13, 14, 15) skeins of 1824 Wool from Mission Falls (100% merino Superwash wool; 50 g [1.75 oz]; 85 yds [78 m]), color 01

Size 9 needles or size required to obtain gauge

Cable needle

4 ring markers

GAUGE

18 sts and 22 rows = 4" in DNA patt

RIB AND HELIX PATTERN
(Multiple of 9 + 5)

Row 1 (RS): *(P1, K1) 2 times, P1, K4, rep from *, end P1, (K1, P1) 2 times.

Row 2: Knit the knit sts and purl the purl sts.

Row 3: *(P1, K1) 2 times, P1, sl 2 onto cn, hold in back, K2, K2 from cn, rep from *, end P1, (K1, P1) 2 times.

Row 4: Knit the knit sts and purl the purl sts.

Rep rows 1–4.

DNA PATTERN

See chart on page 54.

CHROMOSOME PATTERN

See chart on page 55.

BACK

- CO 77 (86, 95, 104, 113) sts and work in Rib and Helix patt until piece measures 4", inc 1 (0, 1, 0, 1) st at end of last WS row—78 (86, 96, 104, 114) sts.

- **Setup row:** Work 11 (15, 20, 24, 29) sts in St st, pm, begin chart for DNA patt, pm, begin chart for Chromosome patt, pm, begin chart for DNA patt, pm, work 11 (15, 20, 24, 29) sts in St st.

- Following charts, cont in established patt until piece measures 12 (12, 14, 14, 15)", ending with WS row.

- **Shape armholes:** BO 8 (9, 9, 10, 10) sts at beg of next 2 rows—62 (68, 78, 84, 94) sts.

- Cont in patts as established, working Chromosome patt 2 (2, 2½, 2½, 2½) times, then work rem sts above Chromosome patt in rev St st until piece measures 20 (20, 23, 23, 24)". BO all sts in patt.

FRONT

- Work as for back, working Chromosome patt 1½ (1½, 2, 2, 2) times, until piece measures 17 (17, 20, 20, 21)", ending with WS row.

- **Shape neck:** Work in patt across 19 (22, 26, 29, 33) sts, join 2nd ball of yarn and BO center 24 (24, 26, 26, 28) sts, cont in patt across rem 19 (22, 26, 29, 33) sts. Working both sides at same time with separate balls of yarn, at each neck edge, dec 1 st EOR 4 (5, 5, 6, 6) times—15 (17, 21, 23, 27) sts each shoulder.

- Cont in patt until piece measures 20 (20, 23, 23, 24)". BO all sts in patt.

SLEEVES

- CO 32 (32, 41, 41, 41) sts and work in Rib and Helix patt for 4", inc 10 (10, 9, 9, 9) sts evenly across last WS row—42 (42, 50, 50, 50) sts.

- **Setup row:** Work 11 (11, 15, 15, 15) sts in St st, pm, beg chart for DNA patt, pm, work 11 (11, 15, 15, 15) sts in St st. Following chart, cont in established patt, inc 1 st at each edge every 4 rows 15 times—72 (72, 80, 80, 80) sts. For better seams, work inc 2 sts from each edge.

- Cont in patt until piece measures 21" or desired length. BO all sts.

FINISHING

- Sew shoulder seams.

- **Collar:** With RS facing, beg at right shoulder seam, PU 81 (81, 81, 90, 90) sts around neck. Join and work in Rib and Helix patt as follows:

  Rnd 1: *(P1, K1) 2 times, P1, K4, rep from *.

  Rnd 2: Knit the knit sts and purl the purl sts.

  Rnd 3: *(P1, K1) 2 times, P1, sl 2 onto cn, hold in back, K2, K2 from cn, rep from *.

  Rnd 4: Knit the knit sts and purl the purl sts.

  Rep rnds 1–4 for 3". BO loosely in patt.

- Sew sleeve and side seams.

- Block gently.

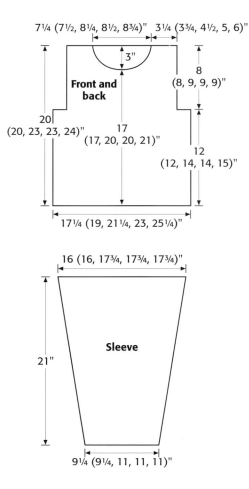

DNA Cable Pattern

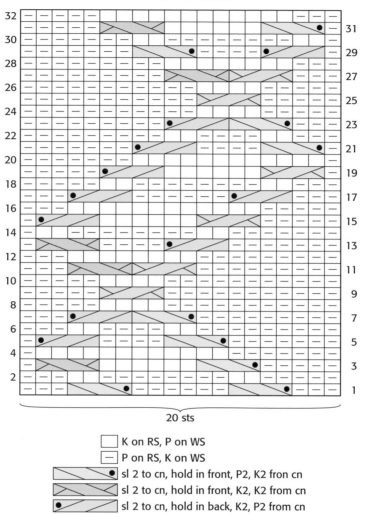

20 sts

	K on RS, P on WS
—	P on RS, K on WS
●	sl 2 to cn, hold in front, P2, K2 fron cn
	sl 2 to cn, hold in front, K2, K2 from cn
●	sl 2 to cn, hold in back, K2, P2 from cn
	sl 2 to cn, hold in back, K2, K2 from cn

Chromosome Cable Pattern

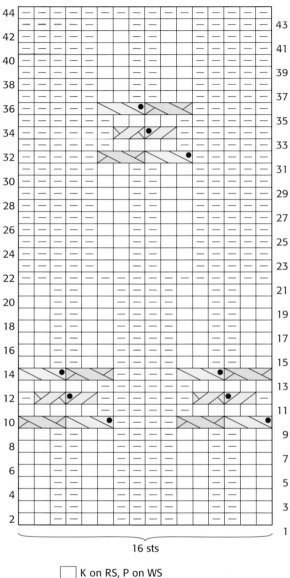

16 sts

	K on RS, P on WS
—	P on RS, K on WS
	sl 2 to cn, hold in front, P1, K2 fron cn
	sl 1 to cn, hold in front, K2, P1 from cn
	sl 1 to cn, hold in front, P1, K1 from cn
	sl 1 to cn, hold in back, K1, P1 from cn

Fences Pullover

It's a classic, with richly textured, fencelike cables;
interlocking lines; and sleek fit.

Skill Level: Intermediate ◼◼◼▢

Sizes: Extra Small (Small, Medium, Large, Extra Large)

Finished Bust: 32½ (35½, 39, 42, 45)"

Skill Builder

Cables: Cables are simply a method for moving stitches across the fabric.
The design is symmetrical; stitches are crossed to the right
on one side and to the left on the other side.

Melissa's Point

I love the symmetry of this cable pattern, and the yarn is light as a feather.
Enjoy an Aran look without the weight.

FENCES PULLOVER

MATERIALS

7 (7, 8, 9, 10) skeins of Via Mala from GGH (100% merino wool; 50 g, 77 yds), color 24 **5**

Size 10½ needles or size required to obtain gauge

Size 10 circular needles (24")

Cable needle

GAUGE

15 sts and 19 rows = 4" in cable B patt on larger needles after blocking

CABLE A
(Multiple of 12 + 13 [7, 13, 7, 13])

C5R (Cross 5 Right): Sl 3 onto cn and hold in back, K2, (P1, K2) from cn.

Row 1 (RS): P3 (0, 3, 0, 3), *P7, K2, P1, K2, rep from * to last 10 (7, 10, 7, 10) sts, purl to end.

Row 2: Knit the knit sts and purl the purl sts.

Row 3: P3 (0, 3, 0, 3), *P7, C5R, rep from * to last 10 (7, 10, 7, 10) sts, purl to end.

Row 4: Knit the knit sts and purl the purl sts.

Rep rows 1–4.

CABLE B
(Multiple of 12 + 25 [19, 25, 19, 25])

C3R (Cross 3 Right): Sl 1 onto cn and hold in back, K2, P1 from cn.

C3L (Cross 3 Left): Sl 2 onto cn and hold in front, P1, K2 from cn.

Row 1 (RS): P9 (6, 9, 6, 9), C3R, *P1, C3L, P5, C3R, rep from * to last 13 (10, 13, 10, 13) sts, P1, C3L, P9 (6, 9, 6, 9).

Row 2 and all WS rows: Knit the knit sts and purl the purl sts.

Row 3: P8 (5, 8, 5, 8), C3R, P1, *P2, C3L, P3, C3R, P1, rep from * to last 13 (10, 13, 10, 13) sts, P2, C3L, P8 (5, 8, 5, 8).

Row 5: P7 (4, 7, 4, 7), C3R, P2, *P3, C3L, *P1, C3R, P2, rep from * to last 13 (10, 13, 10, 13) sts, P3, C3L, P7 (4, 7, 4, 7).

Rows 7, 11, 15: P7 (4, 7, 4, 7), K2, P3, *P4, C5R, P3, rep from * to last 13 (10, 13, 10, 13) sts, P4, K2, P7 (4, 7, 4, 7).

Rows 9, 13: P7 (4, 7, 4, 7), K2, P3, *P4, K2, P1, K2, P3, rep from * to last 13 (10, 13, 10, 13) sts, P4, K2, P7 (4, 7, 4, 7).

Row 17: P7 (4, 7, 4, 7), C3L, P2, *P3, C3R, P1, C3L, P2, rep from * to last 13 (10, 13, 10, 13) sts, P3, C3R, P7 (4, 7, 4, 7).

Row 19: P8 (5, 8, 5, 8), C3L, P1, *P2, C3R, P3, C3L, P1, rep from * to last 13 (10, 13, 10, 13) sts, P2, C3R, P8 (5, 8, 6, 8).

Row 21: P9 (6, 9, 6, 9), C3L, *P1, C3R, P5, C3L, rep from * to last 13 (10, 13, 10, 13) sts, P1, C3R, P9 (6, 9, 6, 9).

Rows 23, 27, 31: P10 (7, 10, 7, 10), *C5R, P7, rep from * to last 15 (12, 15, 12, 15) sts, end C5R, P10 (7, 10, 7, 10).

Rows 25, 29: P10 (7, 10, 7, 10), *K2, P1, K2, P7, rep from* to last 15 (12, 15, 12 15) sts, K2, P1, K2, P10 (7, 10, 7, 10).

Row 32: Knit the knit sts and purl the purl sts.

Rep rows 1–32.

BACK

- With smaller needles, CO 61 (67, 73, 79, 85) sts and work in cable A patt until piece measures 5", ending with row 4.

- Change to larger needles and work in cable B patt until piece measures 13 (14, 15, 15, 16)", ending with WS row.

- **Shape armholes:** BO 3 sts at beg of next 2 rows. Dec 1 st at each edge EOR 2 (2, 2, 2, 4) times—51 (57, 66, 69, 71) sts.

- Cont in patt until piece measures 21 (22, 23, 24, 25)". BO all sts.

FRONT

- Work as for back until piece measures 18 (19, 20, 21, 22)", ending with WS row.
- **Shape neck:** Work across 19 (21, 24, 26, 28) sts, join 2nd ball of yarn and BO center 13 sts, cont in patt across rem 19 (21, 24, 26, 28) sts. Working both sides at same time with separate balls of yarn, at each neck edge, dec 1 st 5 times—14 (16, 19, 21, 23) sts each shoulder.
- Cont in patt until piece measures 21 (22, 23, 24, 25)". BO all sts.

SLEEVES

- With smaller needles, CO 35 sts and set up patt as follows: P2, work cable A 12-st rep from * to * twice, P9. Cont in patt until piece measures 5", ending with WS row.
- Change to larger needles and set up cable B as follows: P8, C3L, P1, work cable B 12-st rep from * to * once, C3R, P8. Cont in patt and inc 1 st at each edge every 4 rows 9 (9, 9, 11,11) times—53 (53, 53, 57, 57) sts. Cont in patt until piece measures 17" or desired length.

- **Shape cap:** BO 3 sts at beg of next 2 rows, dec 1 st at each edge EOR 14 times. BO 3 sts at beg of next 2 rows. BO rem 13 (13, 13, 17, 17) sts.

FINISHING

- Sew shoulder seams.
- **Collar:** With smaller needles and RS facing, PU 72 sts around neck edge, join and work cable A 12-st rep from * to * 6 times. Cont until piece measures 4½". BO all sts loosely in patt.
- Sew sleeve and side seams.
- Block gently.

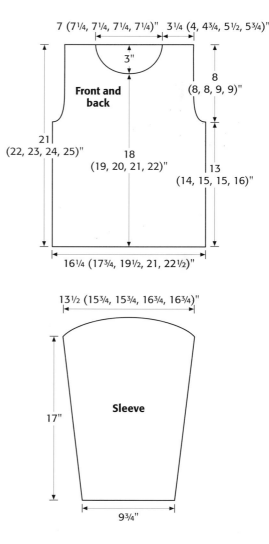

Fuchsia Pullover

Just like the flower, this comfortable-fitting pullover will be a perennial favorite. The Fuchsia pattern is very easy and enjoyable to work.

Skill Level: Easy ◧■□◻

Sizes: Extra Small (Small, Medium, Large, Extra Large)

Finished Bust: 36 (40, 44, 48, 52)"

Skill Builder

Maintaining the stitch count: When you're knitting a lace pattern, the number of increases needs to correspond to the number of decreases to keep the width of the fabric even. The Fuchsia stitch pattern has stitch increases in rows 1, 3, and 5; the corresponding decreases are in rows 7, 9, and 11. Only count the number of stitches after row 11 or 12.

Melissa's Point

This pattern stitch is fun to work and the thoughts of this summer flower will help keep you warm.

FUCHSIA PULLOVER

MATERIALS

6 (7, 8, 9, 10) skeins of Lamb's Pride Bulky from Brown Sheep Company (85% wool, 15% mohair; 113 g; 125 yds), color M23 fuchsia 〔5〕

Size 10½ needles or size required to obtain gauge

Size 10 circular needles (24")

Stitch holder

GAUGE

12 sts and 17½ rows = 4" in Fuchsia patt on larger needles after blocking

FUCHSIA PATTERN
Back and Forth (Multiple of 6)

Row 1 (RS): *P2, K2, YO, P2, rep from *.

Row 2: *K2, P3, K2, rep from *.

Row 3: *P2, K3, YO, P2, rep from *.

Row 4: *K2, P4, K2, rep from *.

Row 5: *P2, K4, YO, P2, rep from *.

Row 6: *K2, P5, K2, rep from *.

Row 7: *P2, K3, K2tog, P2, rep from *.

Row 8: Rep row 4.

Row 9: *P2, K2, K2tog, P2, rep from *.

Row 10: Rep row 2.

Row 11: *P2, K1, K2tog, P2, rep from *.

Row 12: *K2, P2, K2, rep from *.

Rep rows 1–12.

FUCHSIA PATTERN
In the Rnd (Multiple of 6)

Rnd 1: *K2, YO, P4, rep from *.

Rnd 2: *K3, P4, rep from *.

Rnd 3: *K3, YO, P4, rep from *.

Rnd 4: *K4, P4, rep from *.

Rnd 5: *K4, YO, P4, rep from *.

Rnd 6: *K5, P4, rep from *.

Rnd 7: *K3, K2tog, P4, rep from *.

Rnd 8: *K4, P4, rep from *.

Rnd 9: *K2, K2tog, P4, rep from *.

Rnd 10: *K3, P4, rep from *.

Rnd 11: *K1, K2tog, P4, rep from *.

Rnd 12: *K2, P4, rep from *.

Rep rnds 1–12.

BACK

- With larger needles, CO 54 (60, 66, 72, 78) sts and work Fuchsia patt *back and forth* until piece measures 13¾ (16½, 16½, 19¼, 19¼)", ending with row 12.
- **Shape armholes:** BO 6 sts at beg of next 2 rows—42 (48, 54, 60, 66) sts.
- Cont in patt until piece measures 22 (24¾, 24¾, 27½, 27½)". BO all sts in patt.

FRONT

- Work as for back until piece measures 19¼ (22, 22, 24¾, 24¾)", ending with row 12.
- **Shape neck:** Work 9 (12, 15, 18, 21) sts, place center 24 sts on holder, join 2nd ball of yarn and cont in patt across rem 9 (12, 15, 18, 21) sts. Working both sides at same time with separate balls of yarn, at each neck edge, dec 1 st EOR 2 times—7 (10, 13, 16, 19) sts each shoulder.
- Cont in patt until piece measures 22 (24¾, 24¾, 27½, 27½)". BO all sts in patt.

SLEEVES

- With larger needles, CO 24 (24, 24, 30, 30) sts and work Fuchsia patt *back and forth*, inc 1 st at each edge every 6 rows 13 (13, 13, 10, 10) times—50 sts. For better seams, work inc 2 sts from edge.
- Cont in patt until piece measures 19¼" or desired length, ending with row 12. BO rem sts loosely.

FINISHING

- Sew shoulder seams.
- **Collar:** With smaller needles, PU 22 sts along back neck, 7 sts down left front, 24 sts from holder, 7 sts up right front—60 sts. Join and work in Fuchsia patt *in the rnd* for 12 rows. BO loosely in patt.
- Sew sleeve and side seams.
- Block gently.

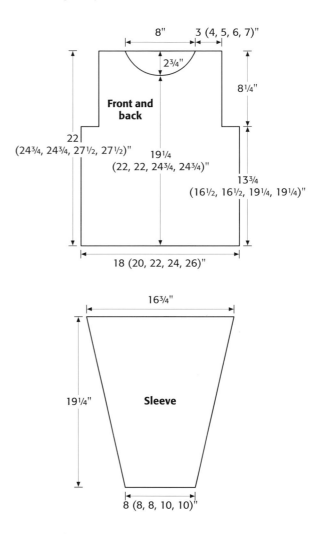

Romantic Ruffle Pullover

*Accented with a ruffle trim and
center lace panel, this buttery soft pullover
will appeal to your romantic side.*

Skill Level: Intermediate ◼◼◼◻

Sizes: Extra Small (Small, Medium, Large, Extra Large)

Finished Bust: 37 (39½, 41½, 43½, 46)"

Skill Builder

K1f&b (bar increase): Knit into the front and back of the same stitch
before slipping the stitch off the needle. This creates a nice,
tight increase without a hole.

Melissa's Point

The front center panel looks like a big cable but it is really
a very simple lace pattern.

ROMANTIC RUFFLE PULLOVER

MATERIALS

7 (8, 8, 9, 10) skeins of Kokopelli from Fiesta Yarns (60% kid mohair, 40% wool; 4 oz; 130 yds), color K24 (5)

Size 10 needles or size required to obtain gauge

Size 8 circular needles (24")

2 ring markers

GAUGE

15 sts and 19 rows = 4" in St st on larger needles

CENTER LACE PATTERN
(Multiple of 18)

Row 1 (RS): P2, YO, K3, ssk, K9, P2.

Row 2 and all WS rows: K2, P14, K2.

Row 3: P2, K1, YO, K3, ssk, K8, P2.

Row 5: P2, K2, YO, K3, ssk, K7, P2.

Row 7: P2, K3, YO, K3, ssk, K6, P2.

Row 9: P2, K4, YO, K3, ssk, K5, P2.

Row 11: P2, K5, YO, K3, ssk, K4, P2.

Row 13: P2, K6, YO, K3, ssk, K3, P2.

Row 15: P2, K7, YO, K3, ssk, K2, P2.

Row 17: P2, K8, YO, K3, ssk, K1, P2.

Row 19: P2, K9, YO, K3, ssk, P2.

Row 21: P2, K14, P2.

Row 22: K2, P14, K2.

Rep rows 1–22.

BACK

- With larger needles, CO 210 (222, 234, 246, 258) sts. Work (K1, K2tog) across row—140 (148, 156, 164, 172) sts. **Next row:** P2tog across row—70 (74, 78, 82, 86) sts.

- Change to smaller needles and work in K1, P1 ribbing for 2", ending with WS row.

- Change to larger needles and work setup row: 26 (28, 30, 32, 34) sts in St st, pm, 18 sts in Center Lace patt, pm, 26 (28, 30, 32, 34) sts in St st. Cont in patt until piece measures 12 (12, 13, 14, 14)", ending with WS row.

- **Shape armholes:** BO 4 sts at beg of next 2 rows. Dec 1 st at each armhole edge EOR 4 (4, 6, 6, 8) times—54 (58, 58, 62, 62) sts.

- Cont in patt until piece measures 20 (20, 21, 22½, 22½)". BO all sts in patt.

FRONT

- Work as for back until piece measures 17 (17, 18, 19½, 19½)", ending with WS row.

- **Shape neck:** Work across 20 (22, 22, 23, 23) sts, join 2nd ball of yarn and BO center 14 (14, 14, 16, 16) sts, cont in patt across rem 20 (22, 22, 23, 23) sts. Working both sides at same time with separate balls of yarn, at each neck edge, BO 3 sts once, BO 2 sts once, dec 1 st at each neck edge EOR 1 (1, 1, 2, 2) times—14 (16, 16, 16, 16) sts each shoulder.

- Cont in patt until piece measures 20 (20, 21, 22½, 22½)". BO all sts in patt.

SLEEVES

- With larger needles, CO 96 (96, 96, 108, 108) sts and work (K1, K2tog) across row—64 (64, 64, 72, 72) sts. **Next row:** P2tog across row—32 (32, 32, 36, 36) sts.

- Change to smaller needles and work in K1, P1 ribbing for 2", inc 2 sts evenly across last WS row—34 (34, 34, 38, 38) sts.

- Change to larger needles and work setup row: 8 (8, 8, 10, 10) sts in St st, pm, 18 sts in Center Lace patt, pm, 8 (8, 8, 10, 10) sts in St st. Cont in patt, inc 1 st at each edge every 4 rows 5 times, then inc 1 st at each edge every 6 rows 4 times—52 (52, 52, 56, 56) sts. For better seams, work inc 2 sts from edge. Cont in patt until piece measures 16½" or desired length.

- **Shape cap:** BO 4 sts at beg of next 2 rows, dec 1 st at each edge EOR 15 times. BO rem 14 (14, 14, 18, 18) sts.

FINISHING

- Sew shoulder seams.

- **Collar:** With smaller needles and RS facing, PU 62 (62, 62, 66, 66) sts evenly around neck edge. Join and work in K1, P1 ribbing for 7". Change to larger needles and work ruffle edge as follows:

  Rnd 1: (K1, M1) around—124 (124, 124, 132, 132) sts.

  Rnd 2: K1f&b around—248 (248, 248, 264, 264) sts. BO all sts loosely.

- Sew sleeve and side seams.

- Block gently.

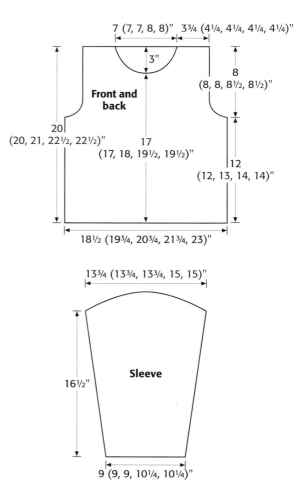

Perfect Sunrise Pullover

This tunic can be worn on or as low off your shoulders as you like. The flowing cables add slimming lines, and the stylish details on the collar bring it all together for a glamorous look.

Skill Level: Intermediate ◼◼◼◻

Sizes: Medium (Large, Extra Large)

Finished Bust: 38½ (42½, 46½)"

Skill Builder

Working vertical stripes with intarsia: Intarsia is a method used to knit isolated areas with different colors or yarns. In this pullover, the collar has vertical stripes made with different yarns. Use a separate length of yarn for each stripe in the collar. Yarns should not be stranded or carried across the back of your work. When changing yarn, cross the new strand of yarn over the old strand.

Melissa's Point

Move over Barbie! You will be picture-perfect and ready to shine in this tunic.

MATERIALS

A 9 (10, 11) skeins of Kid Slique from Prism (66% rayon, 26% kid mohair, 8% nylon; 2 oz; 88 yds), color Tropicana **⑤**

B 1 skein of Bubbles from Prism (100% nylon; 2 oz; 68 yds), color Tropicana **⑤**

C 1 skein of Venecia from Katia (53% polyamide Tactel, 37% rayon, 10% nylon; 50 g; 93 yds), color 08 **⑤**

Size 11 circular needles (24") or size required to obtain gauge

Size 8 circular needles (24")

Cable needle

1 card of elastic thread to match yarn (available at most yarn shops) or approximately 5 yds

GAUGE

12 sts and 12 rows = 4" in Cable patt with A on larger needles

CABLE PATTERN
(Multiple of 46 + 12 [18, 24])

C6R (Cross 6 Right): Sl 3 sts onto cn and hold in front, K3, K3 from cn.

Rows 1, 3, 7 (RS): P6 (9, 12), K6, P14, K6, P14, K6, P6 (9, 12).

Row 2 and all WS rows: Knit the knit sts and purl the purl sts.

Row 5: P6 (9, 12), C6R, P14, C6R, P14, C6R, P6 (9, 12).

Row 8: Knit the knit sts and purl the purl sts.

Rep rows 1–8.

COLLAR PATTERN
(Multiple of 15)

Rnds 1, 2, 3, 4: *With A, P1, K6, P1; with B, P1; with A, P1; with C, K3; with A, P1; with B, P1; rep from *.

Rnd 5: *With A, P1, C6R, P1; with B, P1; with A, P1; with C, K3; with A, P1; with B, P1; rep from *.

Rnd 6: *With A, P1, K6, P1; with B, P1; with A, P1; with C, K3; with A, P1; with B, P1; rep from *.

Rep rnds 1–6.

BACK

- With A and larger needles, CO 58 (64, 70) sts and work in Cable patt until piece measures 17 (20, 20)", ending with WS row.

- **Shape armholes:** BO 4 (5, 6) sts at beg of next 2 rows. Dec 1 st at each edge every 4 rows 4 times. BO rem 42 (46, 50) sts in patt.

FRONT

Work as for back.

SLEEVES

- With A and larger needles, CO 30 sts and work cable patt as follows:

  Rows 1, 3, 7 (RS): P12, K6, P12.

  Row 2 and all WS rows: Knit the knit sts and purl the purl sts.

  Row 5: P12, C6R, P12.

  Row 8: Knit the knit sts and purl the purl sts.

  Rep rows 1–8, inc 1 st at each edge every 4 rows 4 times—38 sts. Inc 1 st at each edge every 6 rows 8 times—46 sts. Inc 1 st at each edge every 4 rows 0 (2, 3) times—46 (50, 52) sts. For better seams, work inc 2 sts from edge.

- Cont in patt until piece measures 16½" or desired length.

- **Shape cap:** BO 5 sts at beg of next 2 rows, BO 2 sts at beg of next 2 rows, dec 1 st at each edge EOR 7 times. BO rem 18 (22, 24) sts in patt.

COLLAR

Prepare 16 strands of B, each approximately 1½ yards long, and 8 strands of C, each approximately 3 yards long. Wind onto bobbins if desired.

- With A, WS facing, and smaller needles, PU sts evenly as follows: 15 sts from right sleeve, 45 sts from back, 15 sts from left sleeve, 45 sts from front—120 sts (this includes picking up 3 extra sts on each of front and back for size Small). Join and work in K1, P1 ribbing for 2½".

- Change to larger needles and work in Collar patt until piece measures 8". BO all sts in patt.

FINISHING

- Sew sleeve and side seams.
- With WS of collar facing you and about 1" from bottom edge, run strand of elastic thread around yoke; join and adjust for personal fit. Work another row of elastic in middle of collar, and one more row about 1" from top. Fold collar toward front and tack in place.

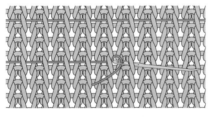

Thread the elastic thread through
one side of every knit stitch.

- If necessary, block gently.

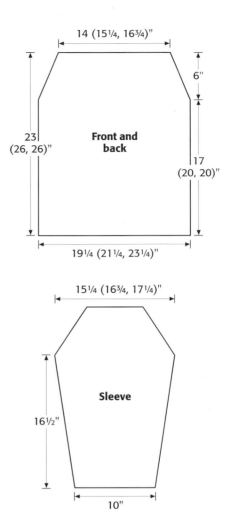

14 (15¼, 16¾)"

6"

23 (26, 26)"

Front and back

17 (20, 20)"

19¼ (21¼, 23¼)"

15¼ (16¾, 17¼)"

16½"

Sleeve

10"

T-Squared Pullover

This sweater is pure pleasure. The precision and rhythm of the T-Squared pattern is a pleasure to knit; the simple, modified drop shoulder sleeves are a pleasure to finish; and the relaxed fit means it's a pleasure to wear. Receiving all the compliments is pleasurable, too!

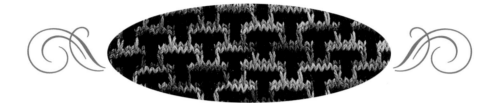

Skill Level: Intermediate ◼◼◼◻

Sizes: Extra Small (Small, Medium, Large, Extra Large)

Finished Bust: 37 (40, 44, 47, 51½)"

Skill Builder

Adding two colors with slip stitches: Slipping stitches is an ingenious way to get two colors in a row while only working with one color at a time. On the knit side, the slipped knit stitch will span two rows in height. On the purl side, the slipped purl bump will span two stitches in width. Block swatch before measuring to determine accurate gauge.

Melissa's Point

This sweater looks much more complicated to knit than it really is. The slip-stitch pattern is nothing more than a simple stripe sequence.

T-SQUARED PULLOVER

MATERIALS

A 2 (2, 2, 2, 3) hanks of Laurel from Schafer Yarn Company (100% mercerized pima cotton; 8 oz; 400 yds), color hand dyed **4**

B 4 (5, 5, 5, 5) skeins Clip from Klaus Koch Kollection (100% cotton; 100 g; 183 yds), color 170 **4**

Size 9 needles or size required to obtain gauge

Size 8 circular needles (24")

GAUGE

22 sts and 26 rows = 4" in T-Squared patt on larger needles after blocking

SLIP RIBBING PATTERN
(Multiple of 4 + 2)

Sl all sts purlwise wyib on RS rows and wyif on WS rows.

Row 1 (RS): With B, *sl 2, P2, rep from * to last 2 sts, sl 2.

Row 2: With B, *sl 2, K2, rep from * to last 2 sts, sl 2.

Row 3: With A, *K2, sl 2, rep from * to last 2 sts, K2.

Row 4: With A, *P2, sl 2, rep from * to last 2 sts, P2.

Rep rows 1–4.

T-SQUARED PATTERN
(Multiple of 10 + 2)

Sl all sts purlwise wyib on RS rows and wyif on WS rows.

Row 1 (RS): With B, K4, sl 1, K2, sl 1, *K6, sl 1, K2, sl 1, rep from * to last 4 sts, K4.

Row 2: With B, purl the purl sts and slip the slip sts.

Row 3: With A, K5, sl 2, *K8, sl 2, rep from * to last 5 sts, K5.

Row 4: With A, purl the purl sts and slip the slip sts.

Row 5: With B, K2, *sl 1, K6, sl 1, K2, rep from *.

Row 6: With B, purl the purl sts and slip the slip sts.

Row 7: With A, K1, sl 1, K8, *sl 2, K8, rep from * to last 2 sts, sl 1, K1.

Row 8: With A, purl the purl sts and slip the slip sts.

Rep rows 1–8.

BACK

- With A and smaller needles, CO 102 (110, 122, 130, 142) sts and work 2 rows of K2, P2 ribbing.

- Work in Slip Ribbing patt until piece measures 2¼", ending with row 4.

- With A, work 3 rows of K2, P2 ribbing.

- Change to larger needles and purl 1 row, inc 0 (2, 0, 2, 0) sts evenly—102 (112, 122, 132, 142) sts.

- Work in T-Squared patt until piece measures 14 (14, 15, 15, 16)", ending with WS row.

- **Shape armholes:** BO 10 (10, 10, 15, 20) sts at beg of next 2 rows—82 (92, 102, 102, 102) sts.

- Cont in patt until piece measures 22 (23, 24, 24, 25)". BO all sts.

FRONT

- Work as for back until piece measures 19 (20, 21, 21, 22)", ending with WS row.

- **Shape neck:** Work 28 (33, 38, 38, 38) sts, join 2nd ball of yarn and BO center 26 sts, cont in patt across rem 28 (33, 38, 38, 38) sts. Working both sides at same time with separate balls of yarn, at beg of each neck edge, BO 3 sts on next 4 rows, dec 1 st once—15 (19, 25, 25, 25) sts each shoulder.

- Cont in patt until piece measures 22 (23, 24, 24, 25)". BO all sts.

SLEEVES

- With A and smaller needles, CO 42 (50, 50, 50, 50) sts and work 2 rows of K2, P2 ribbing.

- Work in Slip Ribbing patt until piece measures 2¼", ending with row 4.

- With A, work 3 rows of K2, P2 ribbing.

- Change to larger needles and purl 1 row, inc 0 (2, 2, 2, 2) sts evenly—42 (52, 52, 52, 52) sts.

- Work in T-Squared patt, inc 1 st at each edge every 4 rows 23 (24, 24, 24, 24) times—88 (100, 100, 100, 100) sts.

- Cont in patt until piece measures 23" or desired length. BO all sts.

FINISHING

- Sew shoulder seams.

- **Neckband:** With RS facing, smaller needles, and A, PU 84 sts evenly around neck edge. Join and work in Slip Ribbing patt in the rnd as follows:

  Rnds 1 and 2: With B, *sl 2, P2, rep from *.

  Rnds 3 and 4: With A, *K2, sl 2, rep from *.

  Rep rnds 1–4 until piece measures 1½". With A, work 2 rows of K2, P2 ribbing. BO all sts in patt.

- Sew sleeve and side seams.

- Block gently.

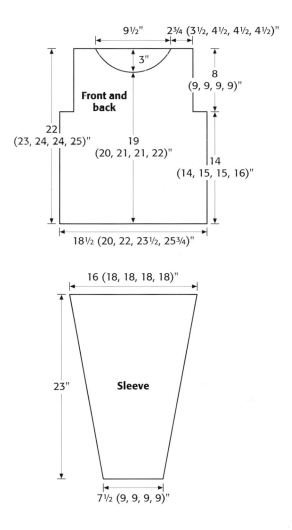

Chevron-Striped Cardigan

Every wardrobe needs a long cardigan with color and texture. This one combines the uniqueness of a chevron pattern with tonal colors and an assortment of yarns.

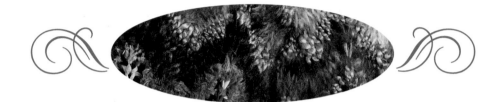

Skill Level: Intermediate ◼◼◼◻

Sizes: Small/Medium (Large/Extra Large)

Finished Bust: 39¼ (52)"

Skill Builder

Changing yarn: The yarn can be carried loosely up the side of the work without cutting; this will reduce the number of ends that have to be woven in. Cross the yarn over at the beginning of alternate rows to avoid long loops between stripes.

Melissa's Point

The yarns in this cardigan came packaged together as a kit for a throw, but I liked them so much that I decided to wear them instead of tossing them on the couch. You will have leftover yarn that you can use to make scarves for holiday gifts. If you'd rather select your own yarns, purchase eight fabulous yarns in different textures and coordinating colors.

CHEVRON-STRIPED CARDIGAN

MATERIALS

One "Absolutely Fabulous Throw Kit" from Colinette, color 19, which includes the following Colinette yarns.

A 1 skein of Zanziba (50% wool, 50% rayon; 100 g; 98 yds), color 128 **5**

B 1 skein of Mohair (78% mohair, 13% wool, 9% nylon; 100 g; 192 yds), color 128 **5**

C 1 skein of Zanziba, color 135

D 1 skein of Mohair, color 60

E 1 skein of Skye (100% wool; 100 g; 163 yds) color 67 **4**

F 1 skein of Wigwam (100% cotton tape; 100 g; 135 m), color 128 **4**

G 1 skein of Fandango (100% chunky cotton chenille; 100 g; 110 m), color 135 **6**

H 1 skein of Mohair, color 135

Size 11 needles or size required to obtain gauge

Size J crochet hook

Purchased clip-button closure

GAUGE

13 sts and 16 rows = 4" in Chevron patt

CHEVRON PATTERN
(Multiple of 10 + 13)

VDD (Vertical Double Decrease): Insert right needle into 2 sts at same time as if to knit, sl to right needle, knit next st, pass both slipped sts over knit st and off right needle.

Row 1 (RS): K1, K2tog, *K3, YO, K1, YO, K3, VDD, rep from * to last 10 sts, K3, YO, K1, YO, K3, ssk, K1.

Row 2: Purl.
Rep rows 1 and 2.

COLOR SEQUENCE

2 rows with A

4 rows with B

2 rows with C

4 rows with D

2 rows with E

4 rows with F

2 rows with G

4 rows with H

Rep for color sequence.

BACK

- With A, CO 63 (83) sts and work in Chevron patt, following color sequence until piece measures 19 (20)" and ending with WS row.

- **Shape armholes:** BO 3 (5) sts at beg of next 2 rows. Dec 1 st at each armhole edge EOR 2 (5) times—53 (83) sts.

- Cont in patt until piece measures 28 (29)". BO all sts.

LEFT FRONT

- With A, CO 33 (43) sts and work in Chevron patt, following color sequence until piece measures 19 (20)" and ending with WS row.

- **Shape armhole:** BO 3 (5) sts at armhole edge once. Dec 1 st at each armhole edge EOR 2 (5) times—28 (33) sts. Cont in patt until piece measures 23 (24)", ending with WS row.

- **Shape neck:** BO 2 sts at neck edge once. Dec 1 st at neck edge EOR 11 times—15 (20) sts.

- Cont in patt until piece measures 28 (29)". BO all sts.

FINISHING

- Sew shoulder seams.
- **Edging:** With G and RS facing, sc along right front, neck, and left front edges.
- Sew sleeve and side seams.
- Clip closure in place.
- If necessary, block gently.

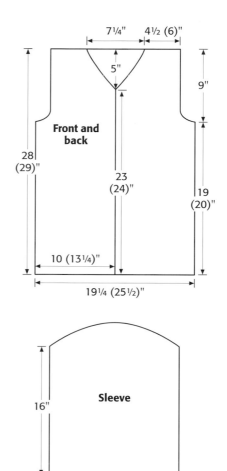

RIGHT FRONT

Work as for left front, reversing shaping.

SLEEVES

- With A, CO 53 (63) sts and work in Chevron patt until piece measures 16" or desired length.
- **Shape cap:** BO 3 (5) sts at beg of next 2 rows. Dec 1 st at each armhole edge EOR 6 (12) times. Dec 1 st at each edge every row 12 (9) times. BO rem 11 sts.

Double-Seed Jacket

Enjoy the relaxed fit and soft hand of this jacket.
The unique yarn is produced by a women's cooperative
in rural Uruguay. Hand-spun and kettle-dyed,
the yarn has dramatic variation in color and texture,
which is emphasized by the Double Seed stitch.

Skill Level: Easy ◖■□◗
Sizes: Extra Small (Small, Medium, Large, Extra Large)
Finished Bust: 38 (41, 43, 45, 48)"

Skill Builder

Working with hand-dyed yarn: Hand-dyed yarns have no dye lots and
no two skeins are the same. To achieve an even color effect, alternate between
two skeins, working two rows at a time from each skein.

Melissa's Point

No need for a closure, as this jacket looks great draped open. But if you need
an excuse for a trip to the jewelry store, a pin would look spectacular.

DOUBLE-SEED JACKET

MATERIALS

8 (9, 9, 10, 10) skeins of Kettle-Dyed Pure Wool from Manos del Uruguay (100% wool; 100 g; 135 yds), color 54 Brick (5)

Size 8 needles or size required to obtain gauge

2 stitch holders

GAUGE

16 sts and 20 rows = 4" in Double Seed st

DOUBLE SEED STITCH
(Multiple of 4)

Row 1 (RS): *K2, P2, rep from *.

Row 2: Knit the knit sts and purl the purl sts.

Row 3: *P2, K2, rep from *.

Row 4: Knit the knit sts and purl the purl sts.

Rep rows 1–4.

BACK

CO 76 (80, 84, 88, 96) sts and work in Double Seed st until piece measures 20 (22, 23, 24, 25)". BO all sts in patt.

LEFT FRONT

- CO 52 (52, 56, 56, 60) sts and work in Double Seed st until piece measures 20 (22, 23, 24, 25)", ending with WS row.
- **Shape neck:** BO 24 (24, 26, 26, 28) sts at beg of shoulder edge. Sl rem 28 (28, 30, 30, 32) sts onto st holder.

Double Seed stitch creates a reversible fabric and a nice finished edge. This allows the collar to be worn many different ways.

RIGHT FRONT

Work as for left front, reversing shaping.

SLEEVES

- CO 40 (40, 44, 44, 44) sts and work in Double Seed st until piece measures 2".

- Cont in patt and inc 1 st at each edge every 6 rows 10 times—60 (60, 64, 64, 64) sts. For better seams, work inc 2 sts from edge.

- Cont in patt until piece measures 16 (16, 17, 17, 17)" or desired length. BO all sts in patt.

FINISHING

- Sew shoulder seams.

- **Collar:** With RS facing, work 28 (28, 30, 30, 32) sts from holder, PU 20 (28, 28, 32, 36) sts from back neck edge, work 28 (28, 30, 30, 32) sts from holder—80 (84, 88, 92, 100) sts. Work in Double Seed st until collar measures 4½". BO all sts in patt.

- Sew sleeve and side seams.

- If necessary, block gently.

Manos del Uruguay yarn is spun from Merino and Corriedale wools and is available in glorious colors.

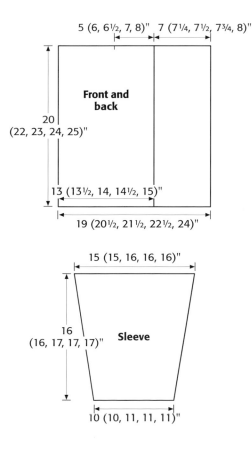

5 (6, 6½, 7, 8)" 7 (7¼, 7½, 7¾, 8)"

Front and back

20 (22, 23, 24, 25)"

13 (13½, 14, 14½, 15)"

19 (20½, 21½, 22½, 24)"

15 (15, 16, 16, 16)"

16 (16, 17, 17, 17)" **Sleeve**

10 (10, 11, 11, 11)"

Pinstripe Jacket

Show your passion for pinstripes with this slim-fitting, zippered jacket.

Skill Level: Intermediate ◼◼◼◻

Sizes: Extra Small (Small, Medium, Large, Extra Large)

Finished Bust: 36¾ (38¾, 40¾, 42¾, 44¾)"

Skill Builder

Inserting zippers: With the zipper closed and working from the front, pin zipper in place. With a sewing needle and matching-color thread, baste zipper in place. Turn garment inside out and whipstitch edges of zipper to garment. Reinforce top and bottom of zipper with extra stitches.

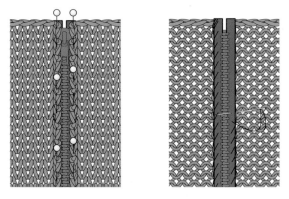

Melissa's Point

Experiment with different colors. I have one of these in black and gold that is very dramatic and dressy. I'm ready for the opera—now if only I had a date.

PINSTRIPE JACKET

MATERIALS

A 5 (6, 7, 8, 9) skeins of Dolcino from Trendsetter (75% acrylic microfiber, 25% nylon; 50 g; 100 yds), color 112 [4]

B 8 (9, 11, 13, 14) skeins of India from Lana Grossa (100% nylon; 50 g; 60 yds), color 17 [6]

Size 13 straight needles or size required to obtain gauge

Size 13 circular needle (24")

Separating zipper 17 (18, 19, 20, 20)" long or size to fit opening

GAUGE

16 sts and 20 rows = 4" in Pinstripe patt after blocking

PINSTRIPE PATTERN
(Multiple of 2 + 1)

Row 1 (RS): *With A, K1; with B, K1; rep from * to last st; with A, K1.

Row 2: *With A, P1; with B, P1; rep from * to last st; with A, P1.

Rep rows 1 and 2.

BACK

- *With A and straight needles, CO 1 st; with B, CO 1 st; rep from * for 73 (77, 81, 85, 89) sts.
- Work in Pinstripe patt until piece measures 4 (5, 6, 6, 6)", ending with WS row.
- **Dec row:** K2tog, K13 (14, 15, 16, 17), sl 1, K2tog, psso, K37 (39, 41, 43, 45), sl 1, K2tog, psso, K13 (14, 15, 16, 17), K2tog—67 (71, 75, 79, 83 sts).
- Work 3 rows even in patt.
- **Dec row:** K2tog, K11 (12, 13, 14, 15), sl 1, K2tog, psso, K35 (37, 39, 41, 43), sl 1, K2tog, psso, K11 (12, 13, 14, 15), K2tog—61 (65, 69, 73, 77) sts.

- Work 7 (9, 9, 9, 9) rows even in patt.
- **Inc row:** K1f&b, K11 (12, 13, 14, 15), K1f&b, M1, K35 (37, 39, 41, 43), K1f&b, M1, K11 (12, 13, 14, 15), K1f&b—67 (71, 75, 79, 83) sts.
- Work 3 rows even in patt.
- **Inc row:** K1f&b, K13 (14, 15, 16, 17), K1f&b, M1, K37 (39, 41, 43, 45), K1f&b, M1, K13 (14, 15, 16, 17), K1f&b—73 (77, 81, 85, 89) sts.
- Cont in patt until piece measures 12 (13, 14, 14, 14)".
- **Shape armholes:** BO 3 (4, 4, 5, 5) sts at beg of next 2 rows. Dec 1 st at each edge EOR 2 (3, 4, 4, 4) times—63 (63, 65, 67, 71) sts. Cont in patt until piece measures 20 (21, 22, 23, 23)". BO all sts in patt.

LEFT FRONT

- *With A and straight needles, CO 1 st; with B, CO 1 st; rep from * for a total of 37 (39, 41, 43, 45) sts.
- Work in Pinstripe patt until piece measures 4 (5, 6, 6, 6)", ending with WS row.
- **Dec row:** K2tog, K13 (14, 15, 16, 17), sl 1, K2tog, psso, cont in patt across 19 (20, 21, 22, 23) sts—34 (36, 38, 40, 42) sts.
- Cont in patt for 3 rows.
- **Dec row:** K2tog, K12 (13, 14, 15, 16), sl 1, K2tog, psso, cont in patt across 17 (18, 19, 20, 21) sts—31 (33, 35, 37, 39) sts.
- Cont in patt for 7 (9, 9, 9, 9) rows.
- **Inc row:** K1f&b, K11 (12, 13, 14, 15, 16), K1f&b, M1, cont in patt across 18 (19, 20, 21, 22) sts—34 (36, 38, 40, 42) sts.
- Cont in patt for 3 rows.
- **Inc row:** K1f&b, K13 (14, 15, 16, 17), K1f&b, M1, cont in patt across 19 (20, 21, 22, 23) sts—37 (39, 41, 43, 45) sts.

- Cont in patt until piece measures 12 (13, 14, 14, 14)", ending with WS row.

- **Shape armhole:** BO 3 (4, 4, 5, 5) sts once. Dec 1 st at armhole edge EOR 2 (3, 4, 4, 4) times—32 (32, 33, 34, 36) sts. Cont in patt until piece measures 17 (18, 19, 20, 20)", ending with WS row.

- **Shape neck:** BO 6 sts at neck edge once. BO 4 sts at neck edge once. BO 2 sts at neck edge once. Dec 1 st at neck edge EOR 2 times—18 (18, 19, 20, 22) sts each shoulder. BO all sts in patt.

RIGHT FRONT

Work as for left front, reversing shaping.

SLEEVES

- *With A and straight needles, CO 1 st; with B, CO 1 st; rep from * for 41 sts. Work in Pinstripe patt and inc 1 st at each edge every 6 rows 8 (8, 11, 12, 12) times—57 (57, 63, 65, 65) sts.

- Cont in patt until piece measures 16½".

- **Shape cap:** BO 3 sts at beg of next 2 rows. Dec 1 st at each edge EOR 10 times. BO 3 (3, 4, 4, 4) sts at beg of next 6 rows. BO rem 13 (13, 13, 15, 15) sts in patt.

FINISHING

- Sew shoulder seams.

- **Collar:** With circular needles and 1 strand each of A and B, *PU 1 st with A, PU 1 st with B, rep from * for a total of 58 sts around neck edge. Work in Pinstripe patt for 1", then inc 1 st at each edge every 4 rows 3 times. Cont in patt until collar measures 4½". BO all sts in patt.

- Sew sleeve and side seams.

- Block gently.

- Sew zipper to front edges.

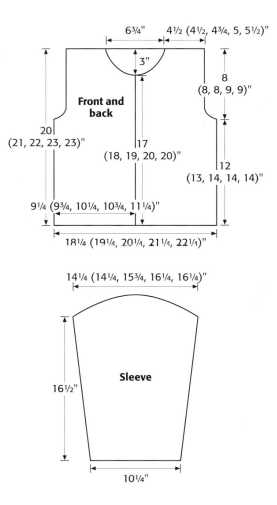

Seventies-with-Taste Cardigan

*The splash of color in the zigzag border is so seventies;
the fashionable flair of the boxy fit is so now.*

Skill Level: Intermediate ◼◼◼◻

Sizes: Small (Medium, Large)

Finished Bust: 35½ (43½, 49½)"

Skill Builder

VDD (Vertical Double Decrease): The vertical double decrease incorporates three stitches into one, leaving a raised row of knitting. Combining the decreases with corresponding yarn-over increases creates the decorative zigzag border.

Melissa's Point

When substituting yarn, make sure you buy a worsted or Aran-weight yarn **⟨4⟩** . The stitch pattern gives a finer gauge than normally expected from this weight of yarn.

SEVENTIES-WITH-TASTE CARDIGAN

MATERIALS

A 11 (12, 13) skeins of Elena from Tahki (100% cotton; 50 g; 98 yds), color 2

B 1 skein of Splash from Tahki (75% polyamide, 25% polyester; 50 g; 114 yds), color 3

Size 8 needles or size required to obtain gauge

Stitch markers

7 buttons, ⅜" diameter

Size H crochet hook

GAUGE

20 sts and 24 rows = 4" in Chevron patt with A

CHEVRON PATTERN (Multiple of 10 + 13)

VDD (Vertical Double Decrease): Insert right needle into 2 sts at same time as if to knit, slip to right needle, knit next st, pass both slipped sts over knit st and off right needle.

Row 1 (RS): K1, K2tog, K3, *YO, K1, YO, K3, VDD, K3, rep from * to last 7 sts, YO, K1, YO, K3, ssk, K1.

Row 2: Purl.

Rep rows 1 and 2.

COLOR SEQUENCE

2 rows with A

2 rows with B

Rep for 28 rows.

BACK

- With A, CO 93 (113, 123) sts and work in Chevron patt, following color sequence for 28 rows.

- With A only, cont in patt until piece measures 16".

- **Shape armholes:** BO 3 sts at beg of next 4 rows, BO 2 sts at beg of next 2 rows, dec 1 st at each edge EOR 3 times—71 (91, 102) sts.

- Cont in patt until piece measures 23 (25, 25)". BO all sts.

LEFT FRONT

- With A, CO 43 (53, 63) sts and work in Chevron patt, following color sequence for 28 rows.

- With A only, cont in patt until piece measures 16", ending with WS row.

- **Shape armhole:** BO 3 sts at beg of armhole edge EOR 2 times. BO 2 sts at armhole edge once. Dec 1 st at armhole edge EOR 3 times—32 (42, 52) sts. Cont in patt until piece measures 20 (22, 22)", ending with WS row.

- **Shape neck:** BO 7 (7, 9) sts at beg of neck edge once. BO 3 (3, 5) sts at beg of neck edge once. BO 2 (2, 3) sts at beg of neck edge once. Dec 1 st at beg of neck edge EOR 8 times— 12 (22, 27) sts each shoulder.

- Cont in patt until piece measures 23 (25, 25)". BO all sts.

RIGHT FRONT

Work as for left front, reversing shaping.

SLEEVES

- With A, CO 73 sts and work in Chevron patt, following color sequence for 28 rows.
- With A only, cont in patt until piece measures 17" or desired length.
- **Shape cap:** Eliminate Chevron patt 4 sts from each end when shaping cap. BO 3 sts at beg of next 2 rows. Dec 1 st at each edge EOR 16 times. BO 6 sts at beg of next 2 rows. BO rem 23 sts.

FINISHING

- Sew shoulder seams.
- **Edging:** Mark buttonhole placement on right front edge. With A, RS facing, and starting at lower right front corner, sc along right front edge, working 1 ch for each buttonhole loop; sc along neck edge and along left front.
- Sew sleeve and side seams.
- If necessary, block gently.
- Sew on buttons.

Design suggestion: Transform this cardigan into a summer shell. Work the pattern as directed, but don't make sleeves. Rather, single crochet along the armhole edge. Wear it buttoned up, leaving the top 2 buttons undone. Purchase 3 skeins fewer.

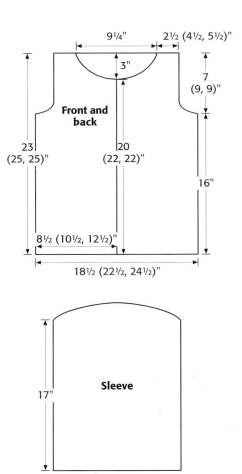

Twists and Feathers Jacket

Birds of a feather may flock together,
but this jacket will stand out from the rest.
The tiny cables can be produced without the use of a cable
needle, and the purchased feather trim adds pizzazz.

Skill Level: Intermediate ◼◼◼◻

Sizes: Small (Medium, Large)

Finished Bust: 39 (46½, 54)"

Skill Builder

Purling into the back of a stitch: From the back, insert the
right needle from left to right into the back of the stitch
on the left needle; wrap yarn around the right needle and draw
the loop through, creating the new stitch.

Melissa's Point

Don't let anyone ruffle your feathers; just enjoy the fun.

TWISTS AND FEATHERS JACKET

MATERIALS

4 skeins of Apollo from Great Adirondack Yarns (50% silk, 50% wool; 160 yds), color Black Orchid 🌀5🌀

Size 10½ straight needles or size required to obtain gauge

Size 10½ circular needles (36") for finishing

3 (3½, 3½) yards of feather trim or other purchased trim

3 sew-on snaps

Sewing needle and matching thread

GAUGE

15 sts and 19 rows = 4" in Twist st patt

For a glamorous alternative, wear the jacket unsnapped.

TWIST STITCH PATTERN (Multiple of 14 + 3)

T2R (Twist 2 Right): Skip first st on left needle, knit into second st through front loop. Without slipping worked st off needle, purl first st through front loop. Sl both sts off needle at same time.

T2L (Twist 2 Left): Skip first st on left needle, purl into back loop of 2nd st. Without slipping worked st off needle, knit into first st through front loop, then sl both sts off needle at same time.

Row 1 (RS): K1tbl, P1, K1tbl, *P3, T2R, K1tbl, T2L, P3, K1tbl, P1, K1tbl, rep from *.

Row 2: *P3, K3, P1, K1, P1, K1, P1, K3, rep from * to last 3 sts, P3.

Row 3: K1tbl, P1, K1tbl, *P2, T2R, P1, K1tbl, P1, T2L, P2, K1tbl, P1, K1tbl, rep from *.

Row 4: *P3, K2, P1, K2, P1, K2, P1, K2, rep from * to last 3 sts, P3.

Row 5: K1tbl, P1, K1tbl, *P1, T2R, P2, K1tbl, P2, T2L, P1, K1tbl, P1, K1tbl, rep from *.

Row 6: *P3, K1, P1, K3, P1, K3, P1, K1, rep from * to last 3 sts, P3.

Row 7: K1tbl, P1, K1tbl, *T2R, P3, K1tbl, P3, T2L, K1tbl, P1, K1tbl, rep from *.

Row 8: *P4, K4, P1, K4, P1, rep from * to last 3 sts, P3.

Row 9: K1tbl, P1, K1tbl, *P4, K3tbl, P4, K1tbl, P1, K1tbl, rep from *.

Row 10: *P3, K4, P3, K4, rep from * to last 3 sts, P3.

Rep rows 1–10.

BACK

- With straight needles, CO 73 (87, 101) sts and work in Twist st patt until piece measures 12 (14, 14)", ending with WS row.

- **Shape armholes:** BO 4 (4, 7) sts at beg of next 2 rows. BO 2 sts at beg of next 2 (2, 3) rows. Dec 1 st at each edge EOR 3 (3, 4) times—55 (69, 73) sts.

- Cont in patt until piece measures 19½ (22, 23)". BO all sts in patt.

LEFT FRONT

- With straight needles, CO 59 (59, 73) sts and work 2 rows of Twist st patt.

- **Shape neck:** Cont in patt, dec 1 st at neck edge every 2 rows 24 (14, 22) times. Dec 1 st at neck edge every 4 rows 10 (14, 14) times.

- **AT SAME TIME, when piece measures 12 (14, 14)", ending with WS row, shape armhole:** BO 4 (4, 7) sts at beg of side edge. BO 2 (2, 3) sts at beg of side edge. Dec 1 st EOR 3 (3, 4) times—16 (22, 23) sts.

- Cont in patt until piece measures 19½ (22, 23)". BO all sts in patt.

RIGHT FRONT

Work as for left front, reversing shaping.

SLEEVES

- With straight needles, CO 34 sts and work 14 rows of Twist st patt. Cont in patt, inc every 4 rows 8 (10, 12) times—50 (54, 58) sts. For better seams, work inc 2 sts from each edge.

- Cont in patt until piece measures 16" or desired length.

- **Shape cap:** BO 4 (5, 6) sts at beg of next 2 rows. Dec 1 st at each edge EOR 14 times. BO 3 sts at beg of next 2 rows. BO rem 8 (10, 12) sts.

FINISHING

- Sew shoulder seams.

- **Neck and front edges:** With circular needles and RS facing, PU 150 (160, 164) sts along right front, back neck, and left front. Work K1, P1 ribbing for 1¾". BO all sts very loosely in patt.

- Sew sleeve and side seams.

- If necessary, block gently.

- **Attach feather trim:** Arrange two rows of feather trim on top of each other so one row of feathers is facing up and other row of feathers is facing down, 1¾" from edge, and with sewing needle and thread, baste in place along fabric edge of trim. Make sure trim doesn't pucker knitting; then sew in place to secure. Fold ribbing forward over edges of trim and tack in place with sewing needle and thread.

- Overlap right front over left front and sew two snaps along bottom of overlapped edges. Sew one snap at neck edge at about bust height.

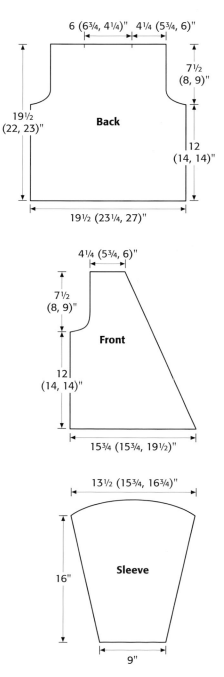

Asymmetrical Poncho

The gorgeous asymmetrical shape is all done
in garter stitch. Wear it with the edge hanging down or
throw it up over your shoulder for a little more drama.

Skill Level: Beginner ◖☐☐☐
Sizes: Under 5' 5", (5' 5" and over)
Finished Measurements: 14¼" x 62" (15¾" x 66")

Skill Builder

Picking up stitches: Insert a needle through both strands of the stitch,
wrap the yarn around the needle, and bring the new stitch through.

Melissa's Point

No sewing required—just knit and wear!

ASYMMETRICAL PONCHO

MATERIALS

5 (6) skeins of Isis from Filati FF (78% nylon, 22% cotton mako; 50 g; 104 yds), color 810

Size 13 needles or size required to obtain gauge

GAUGE

14 sts and 17 rows = 4" in garter st

PONCHO

- CO 50 (55) sts and work in garter st until piece measures 25 (27)"; do not bind off.
- Referring to diagram below, PU 50 (55) sts along CO edge—100 (110) sts. Do not join. Cont in garter st until piece measures approx 62 (66)". To measure, fold piece in half and do not stretch; folded measurement should be approx 31 (33)".
- BO all sts loosely.

FINISHING

- Weave in ends.
- If necessary, block gently.

Garter stitch is made by knitting every row. The fabric is the same on both sides, and the stable edge doesn't roll.

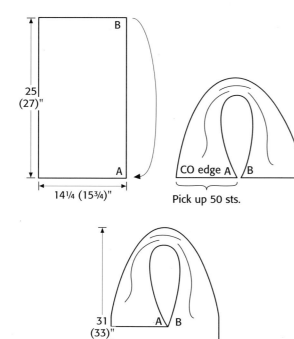

ASYMMETRICAL PONCHO

Red poncho: 7 (8) skeins of Tartelette from Knit One Crochet Too (50% cotton, 40% tactel nylon, 10% nylon; 50 g; 75 yds), color 260

On-the-Fringe Poncho

This poncho is so soft, snuggly, and fun to wear.
Everyone will want one. Good thing it is so easy to make.

Skill level: Beginner ◼☐☐◻

Sizes: Under 5' 5" (5' 5" and taller)

Finished Measurements: 14" x 28" (16" x 32")

Skill Builder

Attaching fringe: Cut the required number of strands twice the desired length of fringe. Fold the fringe in half. Insert a crochet hook in the stitch from back to front. Catch the folded fringe and pull it through knitted piece, creating a loop. Draw the fringe ends through the loop and pull to tighten. Trim the ends as needed.

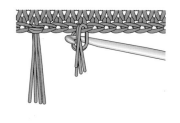

Melissa's Point

If you can make two scarves, you can make this poncho.

ON-THE-FRINGE PONCHO

MATERIALS

6 (7) skeins of Ghost print from Tahki Yarns (100% wool; 100 g; 65 yds), color 4103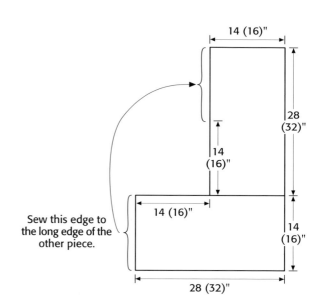

Size 15 needles or size required to obtain gauge

Size K crochet hook

GAUGE

8 sts and 11 rows = 4" in St st

PONCHO (MAKE 2 PIECES)

- CO 28 (32) sts and work in St st until piece measures 28 (32)".

- BO all sts loosely.

FINISHING

- Referring to diagram below, sew short edge of one piece to long edge of second piece. Sew short edge of second piece to long edge of first piece.

- **Fringe:** Using crochet hook, attach fringe around bottom edges (see Skill Builder on page 101).

- If necessary, block gently.

Design suggestion: Make and wear the poncho now. When the poncho craze passes, undo the seams and reattach the 2 pieces at the short ends and you will have a warm and snuggly shawl. Rearrange the fringe as necessary.

Prized Poncho

Cover yourself with color and lines of texture. The innovative approach to this poncho delivers warmth as well as striking looks.

Skill Level: Easy ◼◼☐▱

Sizes: Under 5' 5" (5' 5" and taller)

Finished Measurements: 14" x 23" (16½" x 25½")

Skill Builder

Making tall stitches: Wrap the yarn around the needle the stated number of times for each stitch. On the next row, drop the extra wraps. This allows the vertical threads to form tall stitches.

Melissa's Point

Did you ever think you could knit Koigu KPPPM on size 13 needles and have it look so superb?

PRIZED PONCHO

MATERIALS

A 2 skeins of Zara from Filatura di Crosa (100% wool; 136 yds), color 1404 **3**

KPPPM from Koigu (100% merino wool; 50 g; 175 yds) **1** in the following amounts and colors:

B	2 skeins	color P139
C	2 skeins	color P133
D	2 skeins	color P100
E	2 skeins	color 608D

Size 5 and size 13 needles or size required to obtain gauge

Size 9 needles

GAUGE

16 sts and 7 rows = 4" in Wrap/Drop patt using size 5 and 13 needles

WRAP/DROP PATTERN

Rows 1 and 2: With A and size 5 needles, knit across. Cut yarn, leaving 4" tail.

Row 3: With 1 strand each of B, C, D, and E held tog and size 13 needles, K1, wrapping 2 times; *K1, wrapping 3 times; rep from * to last st; K1, wrapping 2 times. Do not cut yarn.

Row 4: With A and size 5 needles, purl, dropping extra wraps.

Row 5: With A and size 5 needles, purl. Cut yarn, leaving 4" tail.

Row 6: With 1 strand each of B, C, D, and E held tog and size 13 needles, P1, wrapping 2 times; *P1, wrapping 3 times; rep from * to last st; P1, wrapping 2 times. Do not cut yarn.

Rep rows 1–6.

PONCHO (Make 2 pieces)

- With A and size 9 needles, CO 56 (66) sts, then switch to size 5 needles and work in Wrap/Drop patt until piece measures 23 (25½)", ending with row 2.

- With size 13 needles and A, BO all sts loosely.

FINISHING

- Referring to diagram below, sew short edge of one piece to long edge of second piece. Sew short edge of second piece to long edge of first piece.

- Weave in ends.

- Do not block.

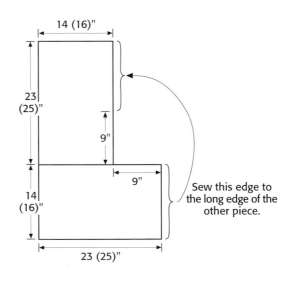

Madison Avenue Poncho

Stroll along Madison Avenue—or any avenue for that matter—in this elegant and graceful poncho with faux-fur trim.

Skill Level: Easy ◨■□□

Size: One size fits most

Finished Back Length: Approx 23" (including bottom trim)

Skill Builder

Adjusting the length: To lengthen this poncho, work additional pattern B repeats; more yarn will be required. To shorten, eliminate one or more pattern B repeats.

Melissa's Point

Be sure to use one color marker for the beginning of the round and a different color for the other markers. I had to use a little nail polish on one of my markers because they were all the same color.

MADISON AVENUE PONCHO   107

MATERIALS

CC 4 skeins of Foxy from Plymouth Yarns (100% acrylic; 40 g; 17 yds), color 06 **[6]**

MC 16 skeins of Cashmerino Aran from Debbie Bliss (55% merino wool, 33% microfiber, 12% cashmere; 50 g; 99 yds), color 300205 (Two strands are held together throughout.) **[4]**

Size 15 circular needles (24" and 36") or size required to obtain gauge

8 ring markers (1 in a different color from the rest)

GAUGE

11 sts and 15 rows = 4" in St st with 2 strands of MC held tog

PATTERN A

Rnds 1–3: Knit.

Rnd 4: *K1f&b, knit to 1 st before marker, K1f&b, sl marker, rep from *.

Rep rnds 1–4.

PATTERN B

Rnds 1–5: Knit.

Rnd 6: *K1f&b, knit to 1 st before marker, K1f&b, sl marker, rep from *.

Rep rnds 1–6.

PONCHO

This poncho is worked from the top down.

- With CC and 24" needles, CO 40 sts, pm (use the one that is a different color from the rest). Join and knit every rnd until piece measures 3". Cut CC.

- Change to 2 strands of MC held tog and knit 1 rnd.

- **Setup and inc rnd:** M1, K14, M1, pm, M1, K1, M1, pm, M1, K4, M1, pm, M1, K1, M1, pm, M1, K14, M1, pm, M1, K1, M1, pm, M1, K4, M1, pm, M1, K1, M1, keep beg-of-rnd marker here and use as mark for inc and for beg of rnd.

- Work patt A a total of 6 times—152 sts at end of last rep.

- Knit 3 rnds even.

- Change to 36" needles and work setup rnd: K28, remove marker, K7, K1f&b, pm, K1f&b, K6, remove marker, K18, remove marker, K7, K1f&b, pm, K1f&b, K6, remove marker, K28, remove marker, K7, K1f&b, pm, K1f&b, K6, remove marker, K18, remove marker, K7, K1f&b, place new beg-of-rnd marker, K1f&b, K6, remove old beg-of-rnd marker and cont knitting to end of rnd—160 sts.

- Beg patt B and work a total of 11 times—248 sts after last rep.

- Knit 5 rnds. Cut MC.

- Change to CC and knit every rnd until trim measures 2". BO all sts loosely.

FINISHING

- Weave in ends.

- If necessary, block yarn gently, but do not block trim.

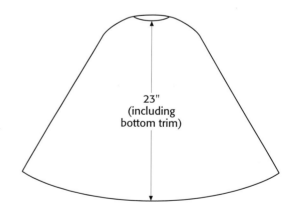

23"
(including
bottom trim)

You'll want one in every colorway.

Olive: Same yarn as model; CC color 05, MC color 503.

Cream: 18 skeins of Merino Aran from Debbie Bliss (100% merino wool; 50 g; 88 yds); CC color 04, MC color 3251.

Useful Information

Whether you're trying to find out what an abbreviation means, what that symbol for "Intermediate" means, or convert meters to yards (or vice versa), the following information should help.

ABBREVIATIONS

approx	approximately		rem	remaining
beg	begin/beginning		rep	repeat
BO	bind off		rev St st	reverse stockinette stitch: purl on right-side rows, knit on wrong-side rows when knitting back and forth; purl every round when working in the round
CO	cast on			
cn	cable needle			
cont	continue			
dec	decrease/decreases/decreasing			
EOR	every other row		rnd(s)	round(s)
g	gram		RS	right side
inc	increase/increases/increasing		sc	single crochet
K	knit		sl	slip
K1f&b	knit into front and back of same stitch		ssk	slip 2 stitches one at a time as if to knit, insert left needle in front of right needle, and knit 2 slip stitches together
K1tbl	knit 1 stitch through back loop			
K2tog	knit 2 stitches together			
m	meter		st(s)	stitch(es)
M1	make 1 stitch (see page 32)		St st	stockinette stitch: knit on right-side rows, purl on wrong-side rows when knitting back and forth; knit every round when working in the round
oz	ounces			
P	purl			
P2tog	purl 2 stitches together			
patt	pattern		tog	together
pm	place marker		WS	wrong side
psso	pass slip stitch over		wyib	with yarn in back
PU	pick up		wyif	with yarn in front
			yds	yards
			YO	yarn over needle

SKILL LEVELS

■□□□ **Beginner:** Projects for first-time knitters using basic knit and purl stitches. Minimal shaping.

■■□□ **Easy:** Project using basic stitches, repetitive stitch patterns, and simple color changes. Simple shaping and finishing.

■■■□ **Intermediate:** Projects using a variety of stitches, such as basic cables and lace, simple intarsia, and techniques for double-pointed needles and knitting in the round. Midlevel shaping.

■■■■ **Experienced:** Project using advanced techniques and stitches, such as short rows, Fair Isle, more intricate intarsia, cables, lace patterns, and numerous color changes.

YARN CONVERSION

To easily convert yards to meters or vice versa for calculating how much yarn you'll need for your project, use these handy formulas.

meters = yards x .914

yards = meters x 1.0936

ounces = grams x .0352

grams = ounces x 28.35

ACKNOWLEDGMENTS

There are so many people who have contributed to this book in so many ways. First, let us thank the talented and gifted staff at the Knitting Tree: Eileen, Liz, Olga, Jolene, and Jackie. Each of you has unique skills, shares your expertise graciously, and is very creative. Thanks for making life so exciting and fun. Second, thanks to all the wonderful customers who encourage, inspire, and motivate. Without you this collection wouldn't have happened. Your support is greatly appreciated.

We thank Martingale & Company for giving us the opportunity to publish. And a special thanks to our technical editor, Ursula Reikes. Your enduring patience, kindness, and diligence are admired and valued. Thank you for your intense work.

Thank you all from the bottom of our hearts.